SEWANEE SAMPLER

By

ARTHUR BEN

and

ELIZABETH N. CHITTY

Arthur Ben Chitty

PROCTOR'S HALL PRESS • *Sewanee*

Printed in the United States of America

*Published by Proctor's Hall Press
Proctor's Hall Road
P.O. Box 856
Sewanee, Tennessee 37375-0856*

International Standard Book Number: 0-9627687-7-4

Library of Congress Catalog Card Number: 78-57385

DEDICATION

TO

HALEY BAIRD CHITTY

who at the age of seven weeks watched
solemnly while his parents, grandparents,
two uncles and two aunts put this
book together.

CONTENTS

Remember the days of old, consider the years of many generations: ask thy father and he will show thee: thy elders and they will tell thee.

Deuteronomy 32:7

DRAGONISH CLOUDS, ELUSIVE VAPOURS

WHEN GARDINER TUCKER compared Sewanee to "A towered city set within a Wood" he probably heard echoes of Shakespeare's *Antony and Cleopatra*. The tragic hero was losing his crucial sea battle to Caesar when he soliloquised:

> Sometime we see a cloud that's dragonish,
> A vapour sometime like a bear or lion,
> A tower'd citadel, a pendent rock,
> A forked mountain, or blue promontory
> With trees upon't, that nod unto the world
> And mock our eyes with air. . . .

Those who have walked through a winter night at Sewanee have seen the same visions Antony saw. In the mists that swirl around crenellated battlements, generations of students have sensed the uncertainties of life the University was preparing them for.

Collecting tales and tabulations, which together might interpret by intimating, has seemed as elusive as "a cloud that's dragonish," mocking eyes with air. When all facts about Sewanee have been assembled in some massive data bank, there still will always be a vapour—something indefinable—which eludes description and must be sensed. If this compilation of the humorous and the serious achieves the goal of sensing, the effort will have been worthwhile.

ARTHUR BEN CHITTY

Fulford Cottage
December 30, 1977
Sewanee, Tennessee

CHAPTER ONE

EARLY TIMES

WHENCE THE NAME?

As early as 1859 the historian William Giles Dix in an address to the trustees of the University of the South said that "Sewanee" came from a Shawnee word connoting "south" or "southern." He pointed out that Indians had referred to the whole Cumberland Plateau and Cumberland River valley as "Sewanee."

In 1953 John P. Harrington of the Smithsonian Institution wrote that the Shawnee Indians inhabiting lands west of the Great Smokies used a word something like "Sewanee" to mean "southern."

The American Indian epic *Walam Olum* (Indiana Historical Society, 1954), an interdisciplinary tome of 379 pages, holds categorically that "Saawaneew" was used by the Algonquian Indians between Indiana and the Delaware coast to refer to "south," the direction in which lived bands of their fellow tribesmen who had migrated seven centuries ago toward the Middle Tennessee and Cumberland Plateau areas.

Walam Olum, or "Red Score," is the migration legend of the Lenni Lenapi (Delaware) Indians as they moved ever so slowly from northeastern Asia, across the frozen Bering Straits, up the Yukon River, across the Canadian Rockies, and down southeastward in a crescent which found them east of the Mississippi River a thousand years later. This book was the product of two decades of study by linguistic, historical, archaeological, ethnological, and anthropological authorities, of whom Dr. Eli Lilly, honorary alumnus of Sewanee, was one.

The *Walam Olum* is—or was—a story painted (Red Score) on sticks and kept in bundles by elders of the migrating tribe. It told in pictographs a tribal legend dating from creation to the coming of the white men to the North American coast. Its scope is comparable to that of the Pentateuch or the *Odyssey* except that its compilers could not write. There are five books or songs totalling 183 verses.

By tragic misfortune none of the sticks survives, but there have been preserved eighty pages of careful notes and illustrations by Professor Constantine S. Rafinesque, a botanist and historian teaching at Transylvania College (1814-1825), who compiled the record and translation in 1833. Apparently the Indians passed on to their children songs which went with the pictographs. These songs were spelled out in phonetic English and translated into original Delaware, then back into English to arrive at the present version. In the process a Delaware dictionary and a Delaware grammar were compiled.

To Dr. Lilly was assigned the task of establishing a chronology based on internal evidence. From his speculations, the Lenapi Indians may have crossed the Bering Sea in 366 A.D., arrived at "Snow Mountain" (perhaps eastern Montana) in 808, crossed the Mississippi about 1000, remaining in Indiana from about 1136 to 1245 and crossing the Alleghenies about 1327. According to Dr. Lilly, those descendants of the original oriental immigrants who had not diverged at the seven points of parting must have arrived at the Atlantic about 1396. Here they may have seen whites "floating in from the north and from the south" in 1625.

Walam Olum in Book V, verses 9 and 10, says: "When Little Fog was chief, many of them went away with the Nanticoke and the Shawnee to a land in the south." At this point the phonetic spelling of the Indian word which referred to this southern region was "Saawaneew." The date here is about 1240 and coincides with the known movements of the Shawnee at the time.

Several other theories as to the derivation of the name Sewanee seem discredited. These theories are that (1) a Creek word Sawani was translated "echo"; (2) a similar word in Shawnee signified "lost"; (3) another similar Shawnee word meant "foggy" or "misty"; and (4) the completely unfounded notion that Sewanee meant "Mother Mountain." Room for speculation on point (3) is provided by the fact that Chief Little Fog was called Tank-awon, the "awon" meaning fog or cloud—(S)awon(ee).

The New York speculators who finished "the steepest railroad in the world" up the mountain from Cowan in 1856 named their firm the Sewanee Mining Company. They would have changed the name of

2

their headquarters to Sewanee from Tracy City had not the alert George Rainsford Fairbanks noted in 1867 that a post office named Sewanee north of Memphis had just lapsed. He applied to Washington authorities before Arthur St. Clair Colyar, the mining company president, heard of the opportunity. Prior to 1867 and on all Civil War maps the present campus area was known as University Place.

Was the name "The University of the South" chosen because it was located at a place known to the Indians as "South" or "Southern Region"? Probably not. There seems ample evidence that the founders chose "of the South" simply to identify the new institution with the self-conscious section about to become, briefly, a nation. The fact that "the South" also had the same meaning to the aboriginal hunters who prized its abundant game is probably pure coincidence.

ABC, edited from *Sewanee News*, February, 1964.

LETTER FROM COLYAR

Colonel Arthur St. Clair Colyar had purposed coming to the Semi-Centennial in 1907 to celebrate his own ninety-first, along with the University's fiftieth, birthday. He could not come, but he sent a letter to be read during the ceremonies, here excerpted.

The early history of the University of the South and Sewanee is intimately associated with that of the Tennessee Coal, Iron and Railroad Company. In 1851 a roving Irishman, Leslie Kennedy, wandered through these mountains and became impressed with the quantity and quality of the coal around Sewanee, and especially around Tracy City. Kennedy went to Nashville and interested a lawyer, Col. W. N. Bilbo, in a scheme to acquire these lands and build a coal road from the junction of the Nashville and Chattanooga railroad at Cowan to this point and beyond.

Col. Bilbo went to New York and interested Samuel F. Tracy and some other moneyed men in the proposed enterprise. A legislative charter was acquired in 1852 for the Sewanee Mining Company for the purpose of mining and selling coal. The money was almost entirely raised in New York, and the railroad commenced in 1853. In 1856 it was completed to what was known as the Coal Bank, which is about

3

two miles from Sewanee on the road to Tracy City. The road was extended to Tracy City in the fall of 1858. Litigation ensued between the contractors and the owners of the property which resulted in two sales of the entire property, one under a judgment from the State Court of Tennessee and one under a Federal judgment in the United States Court. The Tennessee creditors, headed by Col. B. F. McGhee, of Winchester, who was the contractor, bought the property at the Tennessee court sale. One C. A. Proctor, representing the New York creditors, bought the property at the Federal court sale. Soon after this the Civil War came on, and nothing was done with these conflicting claims until 1865, when I went to New York as the representative of the Tennessee purchasers and made a settlement with the New York purchasers, by which the New Yorkers took $220,000 of bonds on the property and turned it over to the Tennessee purchasers.

My father-in-law, Dr. Wallis Estill, and myself were actively interested with Bishop Polk and Bishop Otey in the location of this institution, and the Sewanee Mining Company also took an active interest.

More than 50,000 acres of land had been deeded to this company to induce it to build this railroad, and it in turn deeded to the University of the South 15,000 [actually 5,000] acres of land, known as the Porter, Logan and Estill grants. The title to some of the land was defective, and it was afterwards acquired either by purchase or gift from the people who were the rightful owners. After this site had been selected the preliminary work was commenced. The contract made with the Sewanee Mining Company, when the land was given in 1858, stipulated that, if the school was not opened within ten years from that date, the land was to be forfeited to the Company.

Large endowments were subscribed, principally from Louisiana, and the cornerstone was laid on the 10th day of October, 1860. The day was a propitious one, breezy, bright, and balmy. The whole mountain top was alive with people, more than two hundred bishops and clergymen, in their robes, forming a magnificent procession and marching to the site where the cornerstone was laid, the matchless John S. Preston, of South Carolina, being the orator of the day. There were practically no houses here at the time, and a large crowd was cared for in tents. Dr. Wallis Estill and his family had a tent there. I had a tent, with my family. I remember that Bishop Alexander Gregg of Texas was the guest of Dr. Estill on that occasion.

4

The Civil War came on soon after. Nothing was done until after the close of the war in 1865, which left the whole South in such an impoverished condition that the large endowment fund raised before the war was swept away by the devastation of that terrible strife. The ten years had almost elapsed and the title to the property would revert if the school was not opened. Maj. George R. Fairbanks of Florida had located here in the meantime, and built the famous log house known as "Rebel's Rest." A few days before the ten years elapsed, he and Quintard assembled several boys and formally opened this school, and thereby saved the title to the property.

After the Civil War, I became the owner of the Sewanee mines and commenced the work of rehabilitating the property; and right here I want to bring a charge of larceny against the University of the South. One of the first things I did was to attempt to get the name of Tracy City changed to Sewanee, for the reason that it had been chartered as the Sewanee Mining Company, the coal had been named Sewanee coal, and the mines were known as the Sewanee mines, and we thought, very properly, that the name of the place should be Sewanee. When we applied to the Postoffice Department for a change of the name from Tracy City to Sewanee, we were advised that there was already one Sewanee in Tennessee, and that we could not get the name. At that time the name of the postoffice here was University Place. Upon investigation, we found that there was a little town in West Tennessee, in the Mississippi bottoms, where a postoffice had been established called Sewanee. In a few years, however, that postoffice was abandoned, and the name again became open. Before we found it out, however, Maj. Fairbanks had made an application to the Postoffice authorities at Washington City and had the name of University Place changed to Sewanee.

Arthur St. Clair Colyar, edited from *The Semi-Centennial of the University of the South, 1857-1907. The deed from the Sewanee Mining Company was dated September 25, 1858. The University opened on September 18, 1868, a week before the deadline.*

GENESIS

THE BOARD OF TRUSTEES of the University of the South at its first meeting held July 4-6, 1857, on Lookout Mountain did precisely what other boards do. It orated, moved, perorated, resolved, inscribed, embossed, gave thanks, and adjourned. But then something else happened. The relentless Bishop Leonidas Polk—who had not been presiding officer—began prodding. His letters to Bishops James Hervey Otey and Stephen Elliott, preserved in the Sewanee archives, are masterpieces of diplomacy. Polk was determined that the University not be labeled his personal project, but he was also determined that the plans should go forward. He prompted others to do what he could have done alone much easier.

True to the commitment in their Address issued from Philadelphia, October 23, 1856, the nine signing bishops saw to it that their dioceses were represented at the founding meeting on Lookout, with the exception of Bishop George W. Freeman of Arkansas, then in his final illness. Even Arkansas had its part, for a delegate from Alabama, the Rev. Henry Champlin Lay, soon became bishop of Arkansas.

The official delegates present at the Lookout Mountain meeting— the twenty *de facto* founders of the University of the South—were, from Tennessee, Bishop Otey, Rev. David Pise, Francis Brinley Fogg, and John Armfield; from Louisiana, Bishop Polk, Rev. William Thomas Leacock, George Seth Guion; from Georgia, Bishop Elliott; from Alabama, Bishop Nicholas Hamner Cobbs, Rev. Henry C. Lay, Charles Teed Pollard, and Leroy H. Anderson; from Mississippi, Bishop William Mercer Green and Rev. William Wilberforce Lord; from Florida, Bishop Francis Huger Rutledge; from South Carolina, Bishop Thomas Frederick Davis and Rev. Alexander Gregg; from North Carolina, Rev. Moses Ashley Curtis and Thomas Davis Warren; and from Texas, Rev. Joseph Wood Dunn. Of these men only two, Bishop Green and Gregg, later Bishop of Texas, had any substantial part in the pathetic postwar opening of the University on September 18, 1868. The first three Chancellors, Bishops Otey, Polk, and Elliott, died before the first nine students were admitted.

Every one of the ten original dioceses except North Carolina had a bishop or future bishop present. Georgia and Florida had failed to elect delegates, but their bishops were on hand, and the clerical dele-

6

gate from North Carolina was probably the most vigorous and able priest in that diocese. Taking into account the difficulty of travel and the area covered, it was a gathering without precedent in Episcopal education.

The city of Chattanooga was host to the meeting, and its gift of $434 for food and lodging at Col. James A. Whiteside's Lookout Mountain Hotel was the first corporate benefaction to the University of the South. There are several accounts of the meeting besides the excellent one written into the minutes by Secretary Lay. The choicest of these is by Albert Miller Lea, then a professor at the University of Tennessee, after whom the town of Albert Lea, of Minnesota, is named. Col. Lea was asked by Polk to be marshal of the procession. He wrote this recollection in 1879 at Bishop Quintard's request.

> We wended our way on foot from the city [Chattanooga] some five miles to the Hotel on the Mountain over-looking the plain and river, eighteen hundred feet below. It was a bright summer day, and many dwellers of the valleys joined with the citizens to swell the small but very choice body of delegates. . . .

> The flag was committed to the hands of the gentle boy [eight year-old Herman C. Duncan] and a revolutionary father [who would have had to be over eighty years old] . . . and they two representing the olden time and the young America bore it at the head of the column as we marched from the Hotel to a grove of oaks, hard by, amidst massive rocks, one of which had been elected as a stand. . . .

> Then Bishop Otey, as orator of the day, delivered an absorbing address, in which he inveighed against insinuations that the scheme of the University was born of disunion proclivities. . . . "May the flesh be torn from my arm," he said, "before my hand shall be raised to pluck one star from . . . that glorious banner." As he said this, the flag, which had hung listlessly by the staff . . . was wafted gently by a sudden breeze so as to arrest his discourse until I drew it away. He stopped, held by emotion. The Assemblage, spellbound, held their breath with awe. . . .

The trustees adopted a "Declaration of Principles," all ten of whose policies, in whole or in part, still governed the University at the end

7

of its first century. A statement by Henry C. Lay shows the scope of the thinking of the trustees:

> It was further agreed . . . that the money so raised shall be devoted to securing intellectual excellence rather than expended in material forms. Funds are to be preserved intact. The interest and none of the principal, is to be used in the purchase of lands and the erection of buildings, so that when the university is ready for occupancy its endowments, undiminished, will secure, by liberal salaries, the best talent and the soundest learning that the world can furnish.

And so was concluded the first of six meetings which almost brought forth the first university, in the modern sense of the word, in America. Johns Hopkins, which actually became the first, was still twenty years in the future. These six meetings took eight steps: election of officers, declaration of principles, selection of name and site, obtaining of charter, acquisition of lands, raising of funds, adoption of constitution and tables of organization, and laying the cornerstone. Every one of these steps was made in orderly sequence. Every step was completely successful. A bit more time—and peace—were needed. Both were denied. Two months after the cornerstone was laid on October 10, 1860, South Carolina seceded.

ABC. *On July 4, 1957, the Centennial of the University of the South was celebrated on Lookout Mountain near the home of DeSales Harrison. The flagstaff held a new United States flag, as the original banner was too fragile to be moved from its place on the south wall of All Saints' Chapel.*

FERTILE GROUND

Dr. H. L. Custer has shown us a beet twenty-three inches long weighing over eleven pounds and a sweet potato weighing six pounds and a half. The vegetables were grown at Sewanee on Cumberland Mountain.

Winchester *Home-Journal*, November 3, 1859.

BEFORE THE UNIVERSITY

T HE PRESENT SITE of Sewanee was not on a main Indian trail but lay between two of the north-south routes. One trail came from Altamont across the plateau at Monteagle and down Battle Creek to the Tennessee River. The other came south from Manchester through Estill Springs and Eastbrook and on into Alabama. When the New York-financed mining company came to develop coal banks of the Cumberland Plateau, they chose the indigenous Indian name.

No evidence has been found of permanent settlement by Indians on the mountain-top. Hundreds of arrowheads have been picked up in the vicinity of the University's Hardee Field, adjacent to the big spring successively named for Rowe, Polk, and Tremlett. At one overhang near an eastern edge of the domain, a half-mile past Hat Rock, carbon-tested bones indicate that men were sheltering themselves there on hunting expeditions at the time the Pyramids were being built in Egypt. Down in the valley at Lost Cove Cave, and across the mountain at Russell Cave, it is known that there was continuous occupation by Indians for at least 8,000 years—but not on top of the mountain.

Until 1834 all of the land of the present Domain of the University of the South was owned by the State of Tennessee, although the conveyances for the Shapard tract (near modern Lake O'Donnell) show earlier homesteaders at Sewanee—John Gilliam from 1821, Edward Harris from 1830, and Grandely (or Croudly) Vassar from 1831. In 1834 three tracts of 5,000 acres each were acquired for a few cents an acre by Madison Porter, Thomas T. Logan, and Wallace Estill. Porter and Logan sold their land to the Sewanee Mining Company which, finding little or no coal, gave portions to the University. Estill gave half of his to the University and probably paid for some of the remaining tracts—those of W. B. Shapard (610 acres), Arthur M. Rutledge (410), Abraham Bowers (250), J. B. Hawkins (200), Henry Garner (130), the Decherd family (120), Lawson Rowe (100), D. Barnes (100), Houghton and Hines (80), and Allen Gipson (72).

Early maps of the community now known as Sewanee indicate that it was a place where the Knoxville-to-Huntsville stagecoach road crossed the Cowan-to-Jasper road. Ascending the mountain not far from the point where the Alto-to-Decherd road brushes the base, travellers between 1830 and 1850 came east on the Brakefield Road,

9

past the present University athletic fields. The first opportunity for water was at Rowe's Spring, where a cabin served as an overnight stop and on occasion as a staging point for deer hunters who came up from Salem, Winchester, or Cowan.

Whereas the earlier communities of Franklin County—Salem, Bean's Creek, Cowan—go back to 1800, Sewanee had no resident population to speak of until the railroad started up the mountain in 1852. A map of 1858 shows four buildings at Rowe's Spring, a couple at the present depot site, Barnes' Inn near the present St. Mary's turn of the Sherwood Road (then the road to Cowan), and a hunting shack on the Shapard tract near the present site of Lake O'Donnell on the Jasper Road. It was at Barnes' Inn that Andrew Jackson stopped overnight when he was a circuit judge.

ABC, *Franklin County Historical Review,* June, 1971.

RESTITUTION

A MURDER WAS responsible for the University's securing the tract of land including part of University Avenue and the sites of the Juhan Gymnasium and Hardee Field. It seems that a slave of Lawson Rowe killed a slave belonging to Arthur Middleton Rutledge, who owned a tract of land in the valley. In the settlement, Rowe deeded Rutledge approximately 100 acres of land around Rowe's Spring, later known as Polk, and finally as Tremlett Spring. It was this piece of land which Rutledge gave to the University as part of the original domain, perhaps its most valuable single plot.

Charlotte Gailor, Typescript of a play produced for the Woman's Club at the Sewanee Public School, October 7, 1950, Sewanee Archives.

ROWE'S TAVERN

THE DAUGHTER of Lawson Rowe was born at Rowe's Spring. Her name was Elizabeth Overton Rowe. The Rev. Thomas Gailor Garner has a life-size portrait of his distant cousin who was only about twenty when she died. He also has a sampler dated, he thinks, about 1840,

10

embroidered with a likeness of "Rowe's Tavern." This is probably the earliest visual or pictorial representation of anything at Sewanee.

Thomas Gailor Garner '62 to ABC, San Antonio, November 14, 1975.

THE SHAPARD CHILDREN'S RIDE

From an account by William Booker Shapard, Jr., of Nashville, written twenty or more years after the experience. *He was then living in Opelika, Alabama, where in 1869 he established a bank. He died in 1896. One of the infant daughters, Lavinia Shapard Dowdell (May 4, 1854–January 13, 1916) was the mother of William C. Dowdell, who sent this memoir to ABC, March 30, 1953.*

B Y THE advice of my physician, I spent the summer of 1855 with my wife and two children on the top of Cumberland mountain near where the village of Sewanee now stands.

In September we made arrangements to return to Nashville, packed our few household goods and intended to spend the night with a neighbor in his cabin. Late in the evening Colonel Goff of Nashville and Mr. Ledyard of Mobile came up on the coal train from Cowan depot expecting to spend the night with us, but as our bedding, cooking utensils, etc., were all packed and there was no place in the neighborhood at which they could stay, we decided to borrow a pole car from the railroad and go down to Cowan depot that night. This car was about six feet square. We placed our trunks around the outer edge of the car, leaving a square place in the center, and seated the children in this square, one three years old, the other about 18 months. The balance of the party took seats on the trunks.

The road was new, very uneven, with sharp curves winding around the mountain side and a grade of 135 feet to the mile, from a point near my cabin to the tunnel on the Chattanooga road. When all was ready a Negro man pushed our car about 300 yards to where the down grade begins. I was seated at the rear of the car holding the rope attached to the brake. It was now quite dark. In a short time we came to another car of the same kind on the track, and, as we could not remove it, we changed cars, took the chink from under the car

11

and started again. As I pulled on the brake rope to see how it worked, it came loose. I immediately jumped down and caught the car, expecting to stop it, but in the darkness I stepped on a loose stone and was thrown down. I called to those in the car to throw off a trunk in front. My wife, thinking I was hurt, immediately jumped toward me, and in the excitement of the moment all sprang from the car except the two children and a Negro nurse who was on the front of the car and could not get off until the car had attained such speed that she saw it would be certain death.

As soon as I fell the car started at a rapid rate. I ran after it but soon saw that it was useless. I then returned to my wife and told her there was no hope for our children, as previous to that time several cars had accidently been let loose and after running a short distance had jumped the track and been dashed to pieces among the rocks on the mountain side. I supposed that Betsy, the Negro woman, had jumped off and was lying dead somewhere on the roadside, and even if the car could run through safely (which I considered an utter impossibility), the jolting motion over the rough road would soon throw the children off and that would be certain death.

We tramped along in the dark expecting every moment to find the mangled remains of our darlings. Several times I thought I saw them at the foot of some embankment and after crawling down over the rocks and stretching out my hands to take them up I found I had been deceived by a white rock. At one place I found white clothing from a trunk that had fallen in front of the car and been torn to pieces. No one can form any conception of the agony of that hour, of the feeling of utter helplessness. There was nothing that we or any mortal could do.

There was no hope even if the car should keep the track, and the children should remain on the car until it reached the foot of the mountain nine miles away. There certain death awaited them for the empty cars were always left on the track at the foot of the mountain and the speed at which they were going would break their car into splinters when it struck the empty cars.

Where could we look for help? I had not prayed for years but in the agony of my soul I called earnestly on God to save our children. But it was a hopeless prayer. I never expected to see them again in life.

We at last reached a shanty on the roadside and procured a light.

We learned from the inmates that the car had passed about an hour before at lightning speed and someone on the car was crying murder at the top of her voice. We knew then that Betsy was still on the car when it passed the shanty, but it gave us no hope. The cars at the foot of the mountain were certain death.

Sometime after we left the shanty Mat Williams, the switch tender, appeared around a curve in the road at a trot, with a torch in his hand. As soon as he saw our light he called, "Mr. Shapard, your children are safe in my house." What a thrill ran through our frames. My brain was almost crazed. I ran forward and caught Mat in my arms and gave him a good hug. Then I shoved him off and told him he was a liar,—that it could not be true. Then I made him swear to the truth of it. My wife came up and such a joyful embrace we had. We cried and hugged everybody in the party, and if there had been a dog in the party we would have hugged him too. With our hearts brim full of joy we trudged on to Mat's house, where we found our now doubly precious children fast asleep, unconscious of the danger through which they passed.

The next morning I went up the mountain, picked up the scattered baggage, some of the trunks being found twenty or thirty feet from the track.

Betsy's account of her experience on the trip was very exciting but I have not time to write it now.

BAD BRAKE

A similar ride of almost nine miles down the Mountain on a runaway hand-car in 1911 is described by Ely Green in Ely: Too Black Too White *(University of Massachusetts Press, 1970), pages 136-137. This account is condensed from the handwritten manuscript which may be found in St. Luke's Library at Sewanee. Ely Green, "too black" for the oil fields and "too white" to be a Pullman porter, was fleeing to Cowan to catch a train to Texas.*

W E HAD a hard time getting the heavy cart on the rails. I looked back at Uncle Doss, knowing he had hept me get started away [from would-be lynchers]. The cart moved very slow untill I passed the home of the Sisters of St. Mary, then the grade dropped. I hated to leave these mountains I knew so well. . . . The cart was increasing speed every second. I became worried how could I stay on this flat car going around the curves at this rate of speed. I almost lost my suitcase when it slid away from me. Holding on with one hand I just barely caught the hand-grip with two fingers to hold long enough for the car to straiten, sending it back against me, almost pushing me off the cart. . . . I knew there was no getting off this cart until I was at the end of this track. All at once I knew my life was facing a gamble if I made it. I knew the surges would come from each side. I quickly placed the suitcase in the center of the cart, then lay across it, hooking toes to the side of the cart, holding the other with hands. Soon I was in the bends of the road. It was a struggle to hold on. The cart was flying. I didn't see how it could stay on the track. This lasted for about ten minutes, which seemed like an eternity to me. Trying to look ahead of me it was hard to breathe. I hadnt ever rode this fast even on the train. I cant say that I was scared. Really I didnt care too much about what would happen. I knew this—I am free and my own man. I said several times: I have got to make it. All of a sudden I came out on a rim of the mountain. I saw Cowan below. I knew I had made it. There was one more trying curve almost like a horseshoe bend. This one I had to hold on with my toes. I was tired. I relaxed for a few moments. When I passed over the tunnel of the N. and C. main line I tightened my grip on the cart again. The surge was on stronger than ever. I managed to last it through. Then the road gradually came down parallel to the main line track for a mile. The cart was still traveling at a high rate of speed. I knew I had to stop it some way or jump off before reaching the switch. I had on heavy sole shoes. I chanced falling off by sitting on the edge to press my foot against the wheel as a brake. This checked the cart effectively until my foot was burning painfully. The cart stopped fifty yards from the switch. I tried to get the cart off the track. I couldnt. I knew there wouldnt be a train along until seven o'clock in the morning. I left it and walked to the station wondering why did Uncle Doss put me on a cart with no brake on it. He was a railroad man and knew this road like a book. Did he mean to kill me this way?

BISHOP OF VERMONT

The participation of Bishop John Henry Hopkins in establishing the University and his friendship with Southern bishops were vital factors in the reunion of the Episcopal Church in 1865. An account by his son, John Henry Hopkins, Jr., of the Bishop's survey of the Domain in 1859-60, is paraphrased below.

The Bishops of Louisiana and Georgia, anxious to secure the services of my father's taste in matters of art, offered him $1,500 for six months to be spent there (Sewanee) in laying out this vast property. Bishop Hopkins accepted the offer in order that he might raise the money for a cherished project of his, the establishing of Vermont Episcopal Institute.

Bishop Hopkins arrived at University Place on December 5, 1859. He wrote, "I occupy the best of a set of log houses, in which is the office of Col. Charles R. Barney, the skillful engineer and general manager of the University estate. It is a good large room, with a fine open fire. The logs are hewed smooth, outside and in, and my bed and table are both very comfortable."

The Bishop's cough improved greatly in the healthful air. The water he described as the purest and finest he had ever tasted. "If Lake Champlain could be thrown in," he said, "it would be absolute perfection." The extreme healthfulness of the situation marked it out beyond any spot within his knowledge as the very place for a pre-eminent Church University.

The people around, nearly twenty, young and old, seemed to be much interested from the first in the Morning and Evening Prayer. A few days later Bishops Polk and Elliott arrived, and the three Bishops spent Christmas Day together. Two days later they left, and he never saw either of them again, on earth.

Bishop Hopkins spent about three months in the work of the University, drafting maps of roads and sites, and plans for buildings, and making water-color drawings of striking views.

Having persuaded his Southern friends that in three months he had done all the service that was in his power, he was cheerfully released by them; and sure now of the $750 which would finish the Chapel of the Institute, he sent from Sewanee the appointments for his next visitation in Vermont and rapidly closed his work. At his last Sunday service, on the 25th of February, there were four adults baptized—to three of whom he had for some time been teaching the catechism—and three infants: no small proportion of fruit to gather from so small a flock, though the Sunday congregations had increased to forty or fifty and would have been larger but for the wretchedness of the roads.

From *The Life of the Late Rt. Rev. John Henry Hopkins . . . Seventh Presiding Bishop. By One of His Sons.* New York, 1873. Pages 312 *et seq. A few of Bishop Hopkins' watercolors survived the war. A scene of Natural Bridge is in the librarian's office at Jessie Ball du-Pont Library.*

EARLIEST ALTAR

A DAM G. ADAMS, Florida historian, recalls that the Bishop Polk family altar in Beersheba (pronounced "BURshaba") Springs was moved to the Howell house in 1871. It was then moved to the old hotel (still standing in 1978) where it served as a stand for the water pitcher. It then went to the Burch house which in due course was rented to a merchant as a store, and he used the altar as a meat block.

On a Saturday afternoon about 1950, Sarah Hodgson Torian asked across the street if the Chitties could ride with them in their Buick to Beersheba to get an altar. We went and helped load a truncated obelisk into the back of the car. A few weeks later, after tender care by Lester Finney, there was ready for its place in All Saints' Chapel the beautiful little altar which one sees now in the baptistry. The brass plaque explains that it was before this altar that the trustees at their third meeting gave thanks for the gift of the Charter of the University from the legislature of Tennessee.

Adam G. Adams to ABC, December 12, 1964, with additions from earlier notes. *Near the Polk altar in All Saints' is Bishop Polk's chair from Christ Church Cathedral in New Orleans. These, with the Lookout Mountain flag and its flagstaff, are the earliest links with the University's founding.*

16

CORNERSTONE

The laying of the cornerstone has been thoroughly described by many who were there and some who weren't. Presented here are two items previously unpublished. The first selection is taken from a skit written ninety years later in which ladies talk about the preparations for the affair.

A shed built by John Castleberry was expected to house 300 people. Here were stored 300 pairs of sheets and mattress ticking ready to be stuffed from the twenty bales of hay stacked nearby. The porch was hung with cloth for privacy. Food from one supplier included 284 pounds of ham at 15¢ per pound, 50 turkeys, 40 quarters of mutton, 300 loaves of bread, 150 pounds of butter. Twenty-nine cooks were brought from Nashville—wages $300. Many guests crowded the twenty or so homes in the community, and more stayed at Tracy City (12 miles), Cowan (10 by rail), and Winchester (20). By far the larger number camped in their own tents or slept in wagons and carriages. Four hundred summer guests came from Beersheba Springs, having stayed late in the fall to escape a yellow fever epidemic ravaging the Gulf coast. Carriage driving time from New Orleans was two weeks using four horses. The Rev. Dr. Young, who directed the choir, took 48 hours to travel by train from New York to Chattanooga, then a half-day to Cowan and two hours to get up the mountain.

Charlotte Gailor, Typescript of a play produced for the Woman's Club at the Sewanee Public School, October 7, 1950, Sewanee Archives.

MORE CORNERSTONE

SUNDAY, OCTOBER 7, 1860—At 10:00 P.M. I left for the laying of the cornerstone of the University of the South on the 10th day of October on Sewanee Mountain, Tennessee. Fare to Augusta, Georgia ½—35¢. Arrived in Augusta 11:00 P.M. Omnibus to Georgia railroad depot 50¢. Met there promenading alone Mr. John S. Preston of Columbia, South Carolina.

Monday October 8, 1860—Left Augusta at 12 ½ at night. Fare to

17

Atlanta $5.50. Arrived 10:00 A.M. Left Atlanta 11:00 A.M. Fare to Chattanooga $5.00. Beyond Atlanta a break in the railroad. We had to feel our way sending a lookout ahead around the many curves of this tortuous road. Many on their way to Sewanee got on at different points. Among them, Judge Randall of Florida and ex-governor Johnson of Louisiana who gives $40,000 to the enterprise. Arrived at Chattanooga at 10: P.M. and here we spend the night.

Tuesday October 9, 1860—Hotel Bill $1.50 Fare to Cowan $2.10 with a return ticket. Left Chattanooga at 10:00 A.M. The scenery most of the way to Cowan is wild, mountainous, and picturesque. Arrived at Cowan, a hotel and a depot on a small plain environed by high mountains. At 12 noon we ascended the Sewanee mountain in the cars of the Cowan and Locke City railroad. About 11 miles winding and turning brought us to University depot at 2:00 P.M. Here omnibuses awaited to take us to the University Place about a mile away. Deposited our baggage at the office, took checks and received tickets for our room. Mine was number 12 in number 10 which was the attic of a series of log houses in which were some 50 beds.

Wednesday October 10, 1860—Took a walk on the Corso with Rev. Mr. Glennie. The Corso is a road running around the domain of the University on the brow of the mountain following its angles and is about 30 miles long. At every salient angle a beautiful prospect bursts on your sight. A double log house is University Place. At 12 noon nine bishops in their robes and some 50 or 60 clergymen in surplices and gowns and some 5,000 people formed a procession and headed by a band playing Hail Columbia marched to the spot where the main building of the University was to be. Here Old Hundred was sung by the vast multitude. Each of the Bishops present took part, Bishop Polk laying the stone. Then was sung the Benedicite. Rev. Mr. Young and Rev. Dr. Quintard on opposite sides of the ring singing alternate verses and the whole multitude accompanied by the band singing the chorus. Thence to the large shed seating some two or three thousand persons and the oration by John S. Preston two hours long. Thence to a similar shed to dinner. Speeches from Lt. Maury, Rev. Dr. Barnard, Bishop Smith and others.

Thursday October 11, 1860—Walked about under the trees where the underbrush is cleared out, picked up chestnuts and wonderful acorns for my children as specimens and mementos of what this wild mountaintop is—which is destined, we trust, to bear richer fruit.

Excerpts from the Diary of Rev. John Hamilton Cornish, rector of St. Thaddeus' Church, Aiken, South Carolina, 1846-1869, now in the Southern Historical Collection, Chapel Hill.

PROOF

Two FEDERAL soldiers stole a hand-car for a lark in 1863 and, being inexperienced with hand-cars, started down the Mountain. Accelerating out of control on one of the first curves, it threw them off, and they were killed as they rolled down the mountain into the stream which flows from Bucket-of-Blood Cave. A mountaineer coming along that evening, in the light of a rising moon, dipped up a bucket of water to take a drink and discovered that it was blood red. Then he noticed the corpses of the two soldiers. Hence the name of the cave. The cave flows blood-red water each year on the anniversary of the death of the two soldiers. Dr. McCrady has visited the cave on a number of occasions and has never yet seen the red water, which he says proves that he was not there on the proper day.

Dr. Edward McCrady to ABC, September 15, 1956.

CLIFFS, BLUFFS AND HEIGHTS

Green's View, University View (the Cross) and Morgan's Steep are familiar haunts of today's students, but only the McCradys can locate Croom's and Gregg's Bluffs, Young's Cliff, and Johnston's Height.

From the *Plan of the Lands of the University of the South on the Sewanee Plateau of the Cumberland Mountains 2000 feet above the level of the Sea, University Place, Franklin Co., Tenn.* (about 1870).

BARNEY'S PET

A.T.O. Spring, formerly named Otey's Spring, was in pre-War days called "Barney's Pet" because the colonel, Charles R. Barney, so carefully kept it clean.

Winchester *Home-Journal*, September 23, 1858.

HAWKINS FAMILY

Too little has been printed about the contribution of Franklin County people to the University of the South, not only in recent years but in its beginnings. If one family could be singled out for recognition, it would be the Hawkins family. This would include hundreds of county residents because the prolific Hawkinses married into nearly every family there was to marry into.

Most famous of the clan was Squire Brooks Hawkins, christened exactly thus in 1805 and not acquiring the "Squire" by virtue of membership on the County Court, though he did indeed gain that honor. In later years the proper form of addressing him would have been Squire Squire Hawkins. He and his older brother John Baxter were born in Richmond, Kentucky, and their father Philip in Washington County, Virginia. Squire Hawkins, orphaned at seven, was indentured to his uncle until age 20, at which time it was stipulated that he be schooled for at least six months and taught wool carding and cotton spinning. A year or two before the contract terminated, Squire and brother Jack rode the same horse from Kentucky to Tennessee, and not long after we find Squire living in a house which still stands below the Cross in Hawkins Cove. His land adjoined that of the University in 1858, and he became a close friend of Bishop Leonidas Polk and Col. Charles R. Barney when they were engaged in the pre-War development of the Domain.

Mildred Hawkins Reid and Betty Hawkins Stuart to ABC, February 1, 1972.

HAWKINS TO POLK TO DAVIS

Cowan Tenn

Dear Friend

Having heard but little from you since our seperation in the citty of Richmond so early a seperation I regretted verry much as I desired to stay two or three days there but unexpectely my boys was [moved] . . , I went and seed the battle ground of John Brown I seen the summit on which he paid the debt due him for his folly, and I returned home not satisfied . . . I want to be there but I dont think I could stand the fateege of a camp life but I must see the boys again this fall and stay there for a time provided I can get in to camps. Now sir I [want] you to do two things for me that is 1st give my regards to your family and except the same to yourself. 2nd I would [like] for you to give me letter of introduction and a letter of recommendation to President Davis so that I may be certain to get in . . . as I have no acquaintance in the State out side of camp. If you should [feel] safe in giving me the above letters it may be of great servis to me as I am bound to go back and scout how soon the boys was in the big battle that was fought the other day. . . . I have got no letters from them since. . . . All things are going smoothe about the University place and the country healthy, generally. Now sir I cant expres my feeling whin I saw it announced that you had excepted a position in the army for I was like you thout that the Mississippi Valley was a great link in the chane of defences. May the God that has directed in the past preserve and defend you in the future is the prare of your friend

your respitfulle
S. B. Hawkins

N.B. I understand they are verry strict in camps at Manassa is the acasin I have made this draw on your generosity—yours &c in haste
S.B.H.

Squire Brooks Hawkins to Maj. Gen. Leonidas Polk, July 27, 1861.

21

HORTICULTURE

A FARMER IDENTIFIED as Mr. Caldwell comments on his experience over the previous twelve years raising fruit on the plateau. He had visited the Mountain with Polk in 1861 and established a model fruit orchard near the Domain. Apples did particularly well, he said, with 3,000 trees growing on 60 acres, and specimens receiving prizes at the State Fair in Nashville. Also growing well were pears, plums, cherries, strawberries, raspberries, currants, and grapes.

University Record, Vol. I, No. 4, June, 1873.

CHAPTER TWO

ENVIRONS

Utopian Overtones

THE COMMUNITY of Sewanee stems from two thrusts of civilization—commerce (the mining company and its railroad) and education (the university). Because the university was able to acquire all the land except the actual right-of-way, and because the Tennessee legislature gave unusually broad powers to its trustees, the University came, as was intended, to dominate almost completely the life of the community.

As one looks back historically on what happened in those years before and after the Civil War, one sees that the new settlement hacked out of the wilderness had many of the qualities of the Utopian communities which were such an interesting phenomenon of the 18th and 19th centuries in America. Descending historically from monastic communities (the Essenes pre-dated Christ), these living groups sought in various ways to achieve perfection, usually moral but sometimes economic or cultural. Their classic theme was a faith in human perfectibility, emphasis on environment and education, nostalgia for lost innocence or former imagined integrity, equal distribution of necessities, revulsion against selfish individualism, and withdrawal from the world.

Some of the more famous Utopian projects were Ephrata (Mennonite) in Pennsylvania, one of 130 settlements by small groups from the Low Countries, the Shakers in several sites and the Rappites in Indiana and Pennsylvania. New Harmony, the Indiana venture of Robert Owen, extended hope for economic solutions. Brook Farm was founded to carry out the ideas of the French socialist Charles Fourier. The most famous of all, Oneida, New York, where the attractions of complex marriage (i.e., free love) combined with some successful patents (hunting traps, silver plating) to keep alive a cohesive group.

Obviously, the Sewanee community did not embrace all of the Utopian concepts, but it did embrace some. It had a clearly religious motivation, the idea that the Anglican ethos had something important to say and that it needed a center in which to nurture its ideas and from which to spread them. It would be a mistake to overstress the Utopian quality of early Sewanee but it did (1) choose a place away from the world and seek to fashion a controlled environment, (2) attract to itself and submit to the influence of a small group of strong personalities—Quintard, Hodgson, Gailor, DuBose, (3) devote itself single-mindedly to one "product"—education, (4) enjoy a governance by an absentee board of trustees, and (5) by a natural selection weed out unsympathetic members. (Question: Who would want to come to an isolated village offering no opportunities other than bare subsistence? Answer: only those dedicated to a religious faith and/or its educational objectives.)

Richard William Leopold in his scholarly biography of Robert Dale Owen (New York, 1969) cited four reasons for the failure of the Utopian community at New Harmony, Indiana. They were (1) lack of a consistent program—Sewanee had a consistent program; (2) failure to regulate quality and quantity of participants—Sewanee avoided that because of (5) above; (3) absence of wise leadership—Sewanee's board of trustees, always including ten or more bishops, provided the *sine qua non* of successful administrative continuity, the ability to terminate bad rule; and (4) inability to pay its own way—Sewanee has been able to attract enough external support from the Episcopal Church and philanthropists to offset the internal deficits inevitable to an education operation.

To the limited extent that Sewanee qualifies as a Utopian community, it stands almost alone as one which has thus far succeeded.

ABC, *Franklin County Historical Review*, June, 1971.

A TOAST

By the Rev. Dr. Shoup: "To Sewanee, where people of eminent respectability dwell together in cheerful poverty."

Joseph Brevard Jones '87 to ABC, March 23, 1952.

AFTER THE WAR

W HEN LEE surrendered at Appomattox, Franklin County was not a wasteland as were many communities in the South. Gradually it reassembled the 10,000 white and 3,500 black people who had populated it in 1860. The soil was still fertile. The tunnel near Cowan had not been blown up (a miracle of military failure), and the trains presently began to creep through from Nashville to Chattanooga. All the "rivers" were fordable until bridges could be rebuilt. The 80,000 or so Federal troops who passed through in the summer of 1863 had left roads slightly improved for their own wagon trains. The springs were still flowing.

When the University opened in 1868, many were eager to serve it. Jobs were hard to find elsewhere in the South. Within four years there had assembled along a double-lined street a business community much like the one to be seen today. From the railroad depot up the hill there ranged grocery, bakery, confectionery, restaurant, as well as shops for hardware, tailoring, saddlery, drayage, blacksmithy, and all the services needed at the time. In a few magical months Sewanee became a self-sufficient economic entity. The only essential changes since then have been the substitution of filling stations for the blacksmith shop, the general increase in sales, and the addition of a University-owned supply store on the central campus.

On its western, northern and southern edges, the Sewanee community was bounded by the descending escarpment characteristic of the Cumberlands. Only on the east did it adjoin the private property of independent landowners, mostly farmers. The fresh vegetables and fruits consumed in Sewanee were either brought up from the valley over excessively rocky roads or were raised on the small farms and in the gardens of Bobtown, Garnertown, Tickbush, and the communities out the Sherwood and Jumpoff roads.

ABC, *Franklin County Historical Review*, June, 1971. *Speculators in Tennessee lands advertised in European papers, attracting many superb craftsmen. Whenever Bishop Quintard spotted one, he added to his collection at Sewanee.*

HAYES BUILT

Jabez Wheeler Hayes was the first large-scale benefactor to Sewanee after the war. His gifts were civic improvements in the community. Builder of the first free school, he may be regarded as the founder of the Sewanee Public School, long before the concept of free education had permeated the South. Tennessee did not pass its first compulsory school law until 1907. Hayes may have put as much as $100,000 of his fortune into the early development of the village, most of this before 1875, an amount far above a million dollars in value today.

When Bishop Charles T. Quintard came to the Mountain for the dramatic planting of the Cross in March, 1866, he found left only "an old log cabin," probably a tool shack used by the pre-war workers. This cabin, preserved by George Quintard '79 and long the home of "Aunt Clara," a former slave brought to the Mountain by Bishop Quintard, is now part of the Chitty residence. Everything else was burned. In 1870, when a map of the Domain was lithographed in Philadelphia, there were still only ten buildings in the central "reserve," eleven around the station, and three on the Hayes tract toward St. Mary's. Hayes' home was to become the first St. Mary's convent. By 1872 Sewanee was a thriving community with a village church, St. Paul's on-the-Mountain, seating 250, the Hayes school with 75 pupils, and a Sunday school of 100. Sewanee's leaseholders had increased from 40 to 120 in two years. There were about 30 private dwellings in the campus area and 100 buildings in the village, where the population estimate varied from 500 to 800.

In this rapid expansion Hayes was a key figure. He was born in Newark, New Jersey, on July 8, 1799. In his Northern nativity, he shared with the first and second vice-chancellors and the first commissioner of buildings and lands the distinction of being a Yankee founder of the postwar University of the South. (Quintard was born in Connecticut, Josiah Gorgas in Pennsylvania, and George R. Fairbanks in New York.)

Hayes had no college training. At fifteen he became a watchmaker's apprentice. By 1840 he was a successful jewelry manufacturer. Before the Civil War he had become a civic leader in Newark, a devout Episcopalian, an enthusiastic horticulturist specializing in fruit trees, and an advocate of religious influence in education.

He had heard about the proposal for a great Episcopal university in the South before the war, and when he learned that the idea was to be revived, he took out a 100-acre lease in 1867 on the bluff over Slopewall. For years the puffing Mountain Goat stopped there for spring water while passengers enjoyed a breathtaking view of Hawkins Cove. When Mrs. Hayes died in 1870, he moved to Sewanee. He opened a sawmill, and, according to Fairbanks, "furnished the means on credit for erecting boarding halls and private residences."

The mill was a boon to the growing community. It was located on the stream leading into Lost Cove about a half mile from the station. It developed fifty horsepower from its tubular-flue boiler, had a modern self-setting carriage and a forty-eight-inch circular blade with cut-off saw attached. The same engine operated a planer and a lathe. A shingle machine could turn out 2,000 shingles per hour. There was machinery for doors, blinds, sashes and mouldings. On the upper floor Hayes installed a grist mill. The useful career of this establishment was ended by a fire in 1872, but by then the community had assumed the general appearance it was to have for the next forty years.

Hayes grew a wide variety of choice fruits. He brought in a $2,000 fruit evaporator, according to an 1874 issue of the *University Record*. It could convert 36,000 pounds of grapes into 15,000 pounds of raisins at a cost of 1½ cents per pound, boxed for market.

Jabez Hayes had seven children. His oldest, Mary Amelia, married George A. Mayhew, merchant of the village, and in 1873 they built a large residence behind the present Academy. Their daughter married Troy Beatty '91 who became Bishop Coadjutor of Tennessee.

By the late seventies Hayes was again spending much of his time in Newark, where Bishop Quintard visited him in 1877. The generous industrialist died in 1882, a few months before his 83rd birthday. New Jersey's newspapers hailed him as one of the state's greatest citizens. On balance, he was probably more important to Sewanee than to his home state.

ABC, *Sewanee Alumni News*, February, 1954.

THE DOMAIN

A TTORNEYS FOR the University for years argued that the University Charter not only exempted the University lands from taxation but also exempted improvements on that land. They contended that the language of the Charter "was broad enough to exempt every interest, including the lease-hold interest, from taxation," and that "if the Legislature intended not to exempt" it could have done so in apt terms. Three points are made: (1) Assessment of tax on lease-hold interests (with ensuing sale at public auction in the event of non-payment) would lessen rental value on lease-holds and destroy University income from rents of lessees; (2) Such assessment would deter lessees from leasing the property and erecting improvements; (3) Such assessment of tax would destroy the power of the University to say who shall and who shall not live on its property and nullify the "control of environment" factor which was a pre-condition to selection of the site.

"This University maintains, in effect, a local government, owning all the property and providing in its leases who shall live there and what shall and what shall not be done thereon; it controls the very life of the village." All people living on the Domain are connected with the University. The village is enclosed and kept up by the University. The streets are paved at the expense of the University. This control is so absolute that no municipal government is necessary for peace and good order. Its situation for young men is thus made ideal. The "effect of taking from the University this control, subjecting lease-hold interests of all these tenants to sale for taxes—the opening of this Domain to public purchasers—is too apparent to need discussion." The case was won by the University.

James R. Jetton, et al versus *The University of the South,* Supreme Court of the U.S. October Term 1907, No. 488, pages 8, 9.

This decision was finally overturned in 1969 when Franklin County won the right to tax privately-owned improvements on the Domain. The University continues to supply municipal services such as fire and police protection, though water and sewage systems have been placed in a utility district. The Vice-Chancellor serves as de facto mayor, and a Lease Committee approves building plans and transfers of leases.

RUNDOWN

*S tanding almost alone among early Sewanee documents is the fol·
lowing letter from Miss Sada Elliott—the second woman to receive an
honorary degree from the University of the South. The document was
shown me by her nephew, Dr. Robert W. B. Elliott '94. The asperity
is balanced by the even-handed sprinkling of vitriol in her own house
as well as up and down the present road to the Cross and University
Avenue in the fifth year of their habitation.*

Beginning from the "South End" of town, I will give you the
families as they come. First, the Tomlinsons, who live on the same spot
where the Castleberrys used to live. A square white house with green
blinds, an unlovely porch and not the sign of a shade tree save a few
freshly planted saplings. A straight gravel path leading from a fancy
gate, set in a rail fence, terminates at the foot of a square pair of steps.
This is called "Chestnut Hill", called so because all the saplings are
oak. Mr. T. is very large and fat. He is now doing a thriving
business up here. Willie is under the old man's thumb, in fact, the
only change in the youth is a vast increase in length. He must have
the credit, however, of being fair and square in all his dealings and
of striving against parental authority. . . . Next comes the widow Polk,
a distant cousin of our friends. She is a very nice, common sense,
proper, dignified, kindhearted woman and never meddles in other
people's business. She lives in a melancholy, mulatto-colored, wooden
house with pink blinds, named Waverley. The front yard is trampled
into a desert, only redeemed by the shade trees, a dilapidated rail
fence and no gate. She has three little children and keeps house for
26 boys. Next comes Mrs. Coley's house, which is now occupied by
Miss Gibson and her niece, Miss Jones, with whom Willie T. is "smit".
They have 8 boys. It is quite a neat little cottage, white and green as
usual, a decent rail fence and neat gate. Miss Gibson is "shadily" fifty,
lean and sladderdown, but withal a kindly soul and much liked by
hungry boys. Miss Jones is about Hesse's age, squarely built, but tall
and rather fine looking, a general favorite, but nobody's friend.

Then comes the Turnpike. First on that road is the Dabney family.
Mrs. D. is a large, handsome, loudvoiced, kind hearted, tactless, man-
aging, meddling woman. 2ndly, 6 children. 3rd, Miss Marye, Mrs. D's

sister, a pleasant looking and really fine woman, about Hesse's age and size. 4th, Professor Dabney, a dear, delightful, abstracted, over run, learned, entertaining, over-worked man, delicate, refined and venerable looking, although only 38. Both the Dabneys and Miss Jones are refined. Mrs. Polk is a little western—all lack polish except Mr. D. They live in a melancholy, weather-stained, unpainted, barnlike edifice, named Alabama—in a nice lot surrounded by the usual rail fence. Next comes the Classic Oxford Row, four little cabins, where dwell 8 youths. Next comes the Green's [Lee Porter site], a nice house, out of Downing's architecture, rather variegated in color but generally good looking; named Kendal, flanked by two cottages in which dwell 12 young bipeds. Bishop Green is a nice old man. Miss Lily is about Hesse's age, pleasant enough, not intellectual but not stupid—not graceful and not accomplished—but generally liked. Mrs. Mercer Cotten, her sister, Mr. M. Cotten, and a small baby form the rest of the family.

Next comes Judge Phelan's establishment [Elliott Hall site], a huge ugly, pinky, brown house with pinkier, brownier windows, flanked by two cottages in which dwell 13 young gentlemen. Quite a neat yard, fence, and gate, the fence being plank. The family consist of the Judge, his four daughters and a little rip of a son. The ages of the daughters are rather misty; they range themselves between fifteen and 22—but some inconvenient old family friends who were here last summer put them between 20 and 30. Miss Cilla (Priscilla) is quite handsome, amiable, quite western and unpolished. The next, Miss Mary is smart but uncultivated, spelling "tailor", "taylor", etc. Next is Anne, slender, and sometimes lovely—always pretty, hair like Florence Locke's, gentle, retiring, conscientious, proper, refined, hard common sense, and a fondness for books. She runs the establishment and tries hard to keep order. Next is Carrie, a second edition of Mary, only better looking and more amiable. The Judge is an obstinate conceited old Irishman. Their place is named "The Forks" being situated in the fork, where the depot road [then Tennessee Avenue, but now University Avenue] joins the turn-pike [then University Avenue, now Tennessee]. Opposite the Forks is a dormitory called the Monastery—occupied by Professor Harrison and about seven youths. Next in the same lot lives a Mr. Judd and family. He is a divinity student, was once on the stage. His manner is a little tragic but he is good and

30

self-sacrificing. He has a nice little wife and pretty daughter, like little Phoebe. Next to Mr. Judd come the Elliotts [her own household on the Stiles Lines' site], a very queer sort of family, to tell the truth. They have just moved into their new house, which is quite a decent affair on the whole. The style is Gothic, color pale lemon, trimming white. The lot is quite a nice one though not fixed up yet. On the south side of the big yellow house is a little yellow house, which is occupied by ten youths.

The place is named "Saints Rest". The family are six in number, not counting the baby. 1st is Mrs. Elliott, a most charming old lady of the old school, perfectly indescribable, intensely pleased with and proud of all her children except the second daughter Miss Sada, of whom she is a little doubtful. 2nd is her son "the doctor" a good looking, stiff young man, very well satisfied with himself and all his belongings, but this last seems to be a family trait. He is quite popular and reputed to be scientific and smart. To me he looks as though he were a man who had "tum much oman". He is devoted to his mother, but I think his wife worries him a little. She is too much like an ancient relative of his whom I met once, a Miss Hetty Elliott, in fact, I heard him tell her so once. 3d comes Miss Hesse, she might be termed the "wheel-horse" of the concern; runs the machine and bothers the chaplain, makes him feel queer on the *left side*; Miss Sada called her the "landlady's daughter". 4th comes Miss Charlotte, quite a nice young lady, very highchurch as to theory, has a little too much grecian bend, but generally liked, and very pleasant. 5th comes Mrs. Elliott *secunda*—a commonplace little woman, kindhearted, and amiable, but very fussy and wanting in tact, rather a grooved out mind and wanting in decision. 6th comes Miss Sada—not at all lacking in the family trait of self-complacency, very contrary to every one and everything, and very obstinate—rather selfish and supercilious, quite a tease, not very intimate with anything but her own shadow. 7th comes the baby called generally John, by his loving mama "Jeannet", by his Aunt Sada "Jinny", quite a nice little baby but not quite so wonderful as his adoring mother thinks.

Next to the Elliotts' come the Gorgas family [Brierfield, the Telfair Hodgson house] consisting of the general, commonly called "Old Spot", Mrs. G. and six children, dubbed by Miss Sada, the little "Gorgi" instead of the little "Gorgusses", as they have heretofore been

31

called. The father is a medium sized man, not very pretty, walks "pigeon-toed" and as though on eggs. His mind runs in a straight line, fixed so at West Point, and has never been known to deviate. Mrs. G. is about the same size as the General, not quite so pretty, rather tragic and "soft soddery", walks a great deal with her knees—reminds me a little of Miss Flight, in Bleak House. Four of the Gorgi are girls reminding one strongly of the little Kenwigses in Nicholas Nickleby, their walk is rather a cross between father and mother which makes it a spasmodic creep, they are uglier than both, but quite nice children on the whole. The Chaplain, Gen. Shoup, lives with them—he is as erratic as the clouds—thin, good-looking, smart, pleasant, honest, frank, distracted, and very intimate at the Elliotts, wears long coat-tails, has thin legs and they never go in the same direction, reminds one of a wind-mill.

Next come the Seviers, very kind but rather contracted sort of people. Opposite them lives Mrs. Cotten, a very pleasant woman quite smart, broad minded, sharp tongued, keen, good looking and about 52, keeps Otey Hall [near Walsh Hall]. With her lives Mr. Cooper, a tutor, a very lame man who has to be rolled around in a chair, quite young and an example of Christian resignation and patience to anybody. There is also a Mr. Lee Cotten, called handsome but looks like a barber's apprentice, greasy waving hair that falls poetically low on his brow, "a killing moustache" and bad teeth, keeps a wholesale grocery down at the depot. Then comes the Fairbanks, who live just where the Polks used to. As the Major behaved so gallantly in the war he has named his place, "Rebel's Rest". They are as they were only a little more so.

Next comes the Library [ATO site], then the Holmes family, consisting of Mr. and Mrs. Lucien Holmes and numerous pet canaries. Mrs. Holmes looks like Aunt Emma, rather "wilferish" and has old "Lucien dear" quite under hack. "Old Solution", as the boys call him, reminds one of Chadband and Stiggins, fat, sleek, crawly sort of man, kisses his wife on all occasions, beside all this is a dunder head. Next comes Tremlett Hall [Henry M. Gass site] and the Cook family. Judge Cook a meek, harmless smiling old man, Mrs. Cook a spry little undecided woman, hesitating at everything, but now as my paper has given out, I will desist. You look worn out with all my uncharitable wordiness, but it is all *true*.

Sarah Barnwell Elliott (aged 22) to her brother Robert Habersham Elliott, May 2, 1871. Slightly expurgated by ABC.

PLUMBING

Bathrooms did not rush to the Sewanee scene. Dr. Cameron Piggot, living then in the Charles Keppler house, probably had the first running water, piped downhill from Tremlett Spring. General Kirby-Smith's Powhatan had tub but no toilet. Wigginses at Fulford may have had the first full bathroom, but this is subject to further research. It is almost certain that Mrs. "Buck" Shepherd (mother of David) was the first to have TWO bathrooms. There was no community water system and individuals had their own water storage tanks. Possibly the first underground pipes went from Tremlett Spring to Old Hoffman.

Certain it is that the first showers at Sewanee available to students were provided by classics professor Caskie Harrison in what is now Convocation Hall, first designed as a gymnasium. Some wag said of the noble benefactor, "He has writ his name in water." Other jottings of the time reveal that students swam raw in Hodgson's Pond and at "The Tank", that ladies stored their butter, eggs, and fresh meats at the springs, and that almost daily deliveries could be expected from the valley of wild turkey, squirrels, rabbits, partridges, and occasionally venison.

Dr. Oscar N. Torian '96 to ABC, December 1, 1961. David A. Shepherd '00 to ABC, June 3, 1952. Dr. R. M. Kirby-Smith '95 at sundry times.

MILK-SICK WEED

"**O** RDERED BY the court that Henry Miller at the request of the citizens be allowed to put a gate across the public road leading from the foot of the mountain in the direction of Cowan for the purpose of keeping stock from getting in the Milk-Sick" (weed).

Franklin County Record, 1862-67, May Term 1867, p. 682. *It will be remembered that a scare of Milk-Sickness in Franklin County threatened to induce the pre-War trustees to choose another site for the University. Bishop Polk went to great lengths to allay their fears. Roy Crownover '42 says that there is a Milk-Sick Cove near Sinking Cove.*

CIVILIZATION

"**I** DO BEG you, my dear Major, to have the undergrowth cut out in front of your house. It will give that quarter such a *civilized* look. And with white-washed fences, we shall be able to show a vast advance in morals as well."

Bishop Charles Todd Quintard to Major George Rainsford Fairbanks, July 2, 1868, Sewanee Archives. *The white-washed fences attracted student graffiti as risqué as the era would allow.*

FRESH FISH

ON FRIDAY last Mrs Hodgson sent Mrs Quintard a fine 5 lb German carp taken from ye pond on ye Mountain. This is ye first fish I have known raised at Sewanee.

Charles Todd Quintard Diary, May 11, 1884. *Sarah Hodgson Torian said that fish and typhoid could both be caught from the pond which lay at the end of the ravine now known as Abbo's Alley. The pond was drained when the dam collapsed, described by Ely Green in* Too Black, Too White.

FLESH, FAIR AND FOUL

M R. REUF, the Swiss butcher, would do anything for his friends but nothing—zero—for his enemies. A visitor at Sewanee, unaware of the Reufian way, returned a steak with a note that it could not be chewed. The next day her usual order was not delivered. She, in a pique, ordered her meat via rail from Tullahoma, an expedient fraught with uncertainties. After painful experiences for a couple of weeks she went back to Reuf's doorstep and gave him an order. He only replied, "Why you not get from Tullahoma?" and that ended that. Friends had to order her meat from Mr. Reuf until her penance had been clearly established by a campaign of compliments.

Queenie Woods Washington to ABC, April 15, 1952.

RATES OF EXCHANGE

W HEN I WAS a boy in Sewanee, living there from 1898 to 1908, the farmers used to bring their produce up the mountain, by ox-cart, chiefly from Rowark's Cove. This was before 1900, because shortly thereafter automobiles began to come. Because of the mud holes, the coves and the distant parts of the mountain were not accessible by anything except heavy vehicles drawn by oxen. The trip up the mountain by ox-cart took a long time, and the sight of wagons spending the night in Elliott Park was a common one in all seasons except winter. I remember twice mountain people coming to the back door and quoting the prices of chickens and eggs in shillings. I asked what that meant and was told that there were two kinds of shillings, one the English shilling and one the York. One was worth 16 cents and a fraction (probably 16 2/3 so that six would total a dollar) and one was worth 12 1/2 cents—which was which I don't remember. My mother and my aunts said that in earlier days at Sewanee prices were frequently quoted in shillings.

Charles McDonald Puckette '07 to ABC, October 24, 1952.

LAGNIAPPE

Two LITTLE girls from New Orleans and I went to Wadhams' Bakery to buy some little cakes and candy. When we finished, the elder visitor inquired of Mr. Wadhams, "Where is the Lagniappe?" He asked me, "Queenie, what is she talking about?" I told him she wanted him to give her something for buying the candy. He gave us each a stick of candy. I'm surprised Mr. Wadhams didn't know about it . . . but maybe it was just his Scotch soul rebelling against the foolish custom associated with the Creole culture.

Queenie Woods Washington to ABC, November 14, 1951.

FATE

Prior TO the auto, local public transport on the Mountain was provided by ancient wheeled vehicles known as "sea-going hacks." Most famous of the drivers, a Black who worked for Henry Hoskins, was Mark Fate Williams. French professor John Nottingham Ware once asked Fate whence came his name. The reply was, "I was named for a great nobleman." Dr. Ware was certain that the nobleman was none other than the Marquis de Lafayette—Mark Fate. David Shepherd, who concurred, claimed to have been the last passenger to be driven by Fate in his hack.

David A. Shepherd '00 to ABC, January 3, 1952. Also Dr. John N. Ware to ABC, September 11, 1956.

OIL

John McCrady went walking with a student named Kershaw, General Kirby-Smith, and Miss Sada Elliott. On the side of the mountain they found evidences of oil.

John McCrady Diary, July 25, 1877. *During World War II it is said that a well was sunk near Tracy City striking an oil stratum at such depth as to be unprofitable. The pipe was capped. I saw it one day on a trip to Fullerton's Bluff with Robert Daniel '35 in 1949. ABC.*

DILAPIDATION

W HEN I WENT to Sewanee in 1898, I thought it was the most neglected, dilapidated looking spot I had ever seen. There were very few stone buildings. . . . Dead leaves against the fences had not been raked and there were clumps of bedraggled weeds here and there. In the Chapel yard of old Forensic Hall, odds and ends of wooden buildings used for Grammar School were scattered about looking as if they had been dropped there by chance and had never heard of paint. There was a disregard for material things, for scuffed shoes, or rough side-walks, but each person had the right to be entirely different from any other person. 1898 was the golden era of the old ladies.

Mrs. William Bonnell Hall to ABC, October 12, 1952. *Her husband '86, became professor in the Medical Department and was Vice-Chancellor 1909-14. Their daughter Landon (Mrs. George) Barker is an adornment of the Domain at the date of this publication. The campus described by Mrs. Hall is detailed in a map found in the 1898* Cap and Gown. *One of the wooden buildings in the Chapel yard is nicknamed "Klondyke."*

DIVERSIFICATION

T HE UNIVERSITY PRESS, under the management of Mr. Arthur Watkins, had been newly equipped with types and presses, and newly housed in a sandstone building in 1905. An announcement solicited business from alumni and clergymen for the printing of books, sermons, church yearbooks, orders of service, certificates of baptism, confirmation, ordination, catalogs of schools, colleges, libraries, banks, and general commercial advertising. Newly-printed were the Commencement Address of Baron Speck von Sternberg and Noll's *Dr. Quintard.* The Press would also take orders for hand-made furniture, book shelves, chairs, magazine racks, rugs, tapestries, coverlets, and other examples of home weaving.

The University Press of Sewanee, Tennessee, *Announcement and Catalog for 1905.*

SIGNED

I N THE mountain town of Sewanee, Tennessee, there once lived a man whose hammer and trowel wrought into stone walls the delicate charm of an artist's brush. His name appeared on no building. Yet all who knew his work could find his signature. It consisted of a perfectly round stone visibly but unobtrusively set in each wall.

Mrs. John Martin Taylor, Caldwell, Idaho, to ABC, July 15, 1957. From a pamphlet by Albert R. Barnett. *The man who originated the novel means of "signing" a building was Columbus "Clum" Green. His nephew Glenn Gilliam, also an expert in sandstone, continued the custom in the laying of sidewalks. See especially the round stones in the walks in front of the Juhan Gymnasium, the duPont Library, and the Woods Laboratories.*

NO DISRESPECT

A SMALL MALE child was brought to Otey Parish church to be baptized. The Rev. Haskell DuBose recognized the father, Mr. Gudger, as one who presented an infant regularly, about once a year. When Dr. DuBose said "Name this child," the parent said, *"Doctor Lawton Wiggins Gudger."* Dr. DuBose went on with the ceremony, but at the moment of christening omitted the "Doctor.'" Gudger stopped him. "You call him Doctor Lawton Wiggins Gudger, or you won't sprinkle him nary a drop." Next year came another Gudger infant, this time female. "Name this child, etc. . ." and the reply, "Miss Lily Green Gudger." Haskell should have known better but he inquired, "Why Miss?" Gudger with great dignity responded with a rhetorical question: "Do you think I'd be disrespectful to a notorious lady like Miss Lily Green?"

Mary Marrs to Fanny deRosset, July 19, 1954. Also J. N. Ware to ABC, September 11, 1956. *Elizabeth Waters Green (1847-1917) is memorialized in the Lily Green Guild at Otey Parish. Her only rival in christenings was Miss Flora Fairbanks (1848-1931), whose tablet reads, "Her 286 God children rise up and call her blessed."*

MOFFAT, TENNESSEE

Everyone knows that Monteagle, five miles from Sewanee, was named for the English Lord Monteagle and is pronounced with accent on the first, not second, syllable. Only a few know that it was first called Moffat.

John Moffat was born in Glasgow on November 9, 1828. He died on Christmas Day, 1886, in Monteagle. His family brought him from Scotland to Canada as a small child, and the father disappeared. At seven John was adopted by Canadians. He worked his way through college by teaching English. He married Lydia Landon, born July 4, 1829, in Canada of American parents. By 1858 he was absorbed in the temperance movement, touring the U.S. as a lecturer. He had two sons, Henry and John, and three daughters, Jane, Mary Adelene, and Lillian. Moffat retired from lecturing, bought a tract of land from bluff to bluff, five miles from Sewanee, and moved there in 1871. He became division manager for the Tennessee Immigration, Labor, and Real Estate Association. Governor James D. Porter appointed him Commissioner for Immigration in 1875, and he was active in promoting the sale of the Gruetli property to the Swiss settlers. In about 1872 he gave fifty acres of land to Mrs. Mary Louise Yerger and Mrs. Harriet B. Kells, enabling them to move their school from Mississippi. He also constructed the first building for Fairmount School, which opened April 9, 1873, with ten girls, and to which William Porcher DuBose commuted by train from Sewanee to serve as chaplain, later marrying Mrs. Yerger.

From Philip Butcher, *George Washington Cable* (New York: Columbia University Press, 1959), pages 65-70.

In Monteagle each summer the Monteagle Sunday School Assembly operates in the cultural tradition of the Chautauqua movement of the 1880's. Victorian cottages on leased land draw third and fourth generation Assembly members for lectures, concerts and twilight prayers.

BOTTLED BEVERAGE

Before Coca-Cola swept the land, small bottling companies, stealing the idea from Cuba, sold sweet-flavored drinks called "pop." In the 1960's, in a ditch behind Chief Matlock's place on the old Cowan Road, Bruce Waggoner, now deceased, found a brown, seven-ounce, glass embossed "Gayola—Winchester, Tennessee."

It set local historians scurrying. Up came this vignette. Charles Gonsolin worked for Pat Jones' plant about 1910, and when the week's Gayola had been diluted and bottled, the entire personnel of the plant (three or four males) would fill the mixing tank and take their weekly bath in it. Presumably they would rinse the tank afterward, before mixing the next week's Gayola, but no one has ever been able to establish whether or not they washed the tank, or how well.

Gladys Waggoner to ABC, January 11, 1972.

BUILDING THE CROSS

The first work done on the Memorial Cross at University View was during my freshman year, the fall of 1921. Dr. Ben Finney gave a talk in chapel one morning, describing the community of interest which existed between the University and the people of Franklin County, and invited the student body to repair to the site to gather stones for the foundation of the proposed Memorial. There was an almost unanimous turn-out of the student body. There were wagons supplied by county people into which we piled rocks. There was certainly in my own heart and mind a strong feeling of participation in this memorial to the men who had fought for our country.

Cameron M. Plummer '25 to ABC, June 15, 1956. *Endowment for the electric bill for lighting the Cross was provided by the first edition of the* Sewanee Cook Book, *edited by Queenie Woods Washington. Subsequent editions have lighted Shapard Tower and now provide contributions to Emerald-Hodgson Hospital.*

AMBULANCE SERVICE

T HE OLD Squire Brooks Hawkins home, at the head of the cove and at the foot of the Mountain below University View, changed hands after Squire's death in 1871. His son Sam bought it from the other heirs in 1909, sold it to V. H. Hinch, he to Sam Farris, and he to James R. Miller '45 in 1967. The house stood on the old stagecoach road which would get so bad in wet weather that when a doctor from Sewanee around the turn of the century came to make a house call, he would ride to see his patient. Once a Hawkins got sick in winter and was put on a cot, with hot bricks around to keep him warm, and eight neighbors taking turns carried him up the mountain on foot to the Sewanee hospital.

Miss Cletus Garner, 1969, Sewanee Archives.

SUPPLYING AND STORE-ING

T HE HAWKINS dynasty at the Supply Store began before World War I with the employment of Hilarius "Hoss" Hawkins. Ignorant students thought his name was hilarious, not recognizing the Latin name of St. Hilary, pope from 461 to 468. In 1917 Hoss was joined by brother Jack and the following year by brother Tom. Hoss died in 1944, and Tom retired after 47 years. Hoss opened the store each day, looking after groceries and soda fountain. Jack handled stock and twice-daily deliveries. Tom's stationery department included textbooks, shoes, caps and gowns. Jack's son Jack and Tom's son Hub came aboard during World War II. Hub presides over "University Market" now, with Jack in charge of meat. From time to time other Hawkinses came and went: Joe, now in Atlanta, Betty (Mrs. John Stuart) and Mildred (Mrs. Carl Reid). Man-hours of service to the "Supe Store" we decline to compute, but person-years would come to more than 200.

Mildred Reid, Jack, Jr., and Herbert Hawkins to ABC in assorted conversations, 1970-78.

SPELEOLOGY

WITHIN SEVENTY-FIVE miles of Sewanee there are sequestered more caves than anywhere else in America. If you don't believe it, ask Fritz Whitesell. He will show you the book.

Although the local populace in the last century and a half has penetrated most of them, a virgin occasionally is unveiled. Peebles Cave, first entered by Edward McCrady Peebles '49, comes to mind. Such speleological exhilaration, however, is reserved for a few. This writer is fortunate to be among their number. Seems that veteran crawler Harvey Templeton, or maybe it was Henry Kirby-Smith, heard that the little pool of water at the far end of Salt River Cave in Sinking Cove had a veritable blast of wind coming from behind it. That, of course, indicated that there must be a chimney beyond, and, if so, there might be an unexplored cave. The party, if I recall correctly, included Harvey, Henry, Robert Daniel, Doug Vaughan, and me. We provided ourselves with the usual carbide lamps and the not-so-usual inflated inner tubes and a long rope. If wet suits had been invented by then, nobody had one. We shivered in the fifty-five degree water found uniformly in Tennessee caves. We swam in under a rock ceiling at times only six inches above the little lake. No one could touch bottom even by diving. After two hundred or maybe three hundred feet the rock floor could be felt, and we waded into a rather large and beautiful chamber. There was absolutely no evidence that it had ever been entered before. No initials on walls, no broken rock formations, no footprints in sand. Coming out, the indefatigable Templeton was crawling under a low ceiling at our flank, and he called out, "Bring some light." We did, and we saw a little chamber not much bigger than a coffin, barred like an animal's cage with two-foot stalactites. Harvey broke a half-dozen of them and wriggled in to see if there really might be a skeleton. There was. It was partly in mud and partly exposed. Even on the spot we could tell it was probably a five-foot-long cat. My very own sweat shirt provided the bag in which it was taken to the biology lab for Ned McCrady's inspection. I can't remember whether it was this feline, mistakenly labelled "tiger" by the press, or the one from the Sparta cave, which finally went to the Smithsonian as the largest and best preserved pre-historic cat find east of the Mississippi. Of course, the asphalt lakes of the West hold the

42

American record for skeletal productivity. Even though it didn't get us into the Guinness Book, we all felt speleologically fulfilled.

ABC, assorted notes and recollections.

THE GARNERS

It was probably in 1946 when I was summoned, as director of public relations, to the Emerald-Hodgson Hospital by the late Harrold Rae Flintoff '35, the superintendent. He had a patient he thought I should meet. Miss Mucidore Garner, an eighty-four-year-old wisp of a lady, was perched on her bed in private room number 5.

Where was she from? Lost Cove. How long had she lived there? Born there. Where had her parents come from? The other side of the Mountain. How many times had she previously visited Sewanee? Never before. (The distance as the crow flies is five miles).

Why had she come to the hospital—what were her symptoms? She was tired. How had she realized it was time to seek medical aid? It was the first time in her life she had not been able to do the spring plowing. How had she gotten to the hospital? Nephews had carried her up the mountain-side to Natural Bridge with two poles and a blanket, and they had been met by a pick-up truck from Sherwood.

Then she did go frequently the five miles to Sherwood? Oh, no, only two or three times. Had she ever been to more distant places? Yes. Where? To Decherd on the train. What had she done when she got there? Came back on the next train. Had she ever had her picture taken? No.

Rex Pinson, subsequently valedictorian of the class of 1948, shot a couple of poses with his 4x5 Speed Graphic, and I promised to bring copies to her. There was a delay of a few days, and when I got back to the hospital, she had conquered that tired feeling sufficiently to go home. I set out for Lost Cove, an eighteen-thousand-acre valley-bottom shut from the world by "The Saddle," a 600-foot ridge lying athwart what normally would have been the open end of the Cove. Under the Saddle, as every Sewanee speleologist knows, flows the beautiful stream that made Lost Cove Cave a deluxe hotel for Indians 8,000 years ago.

I went down as she had come up, via Natural Bridge, found the stream and followed it a mile or so to the dog-trot cabin where Miss Mucidore lived with the only other two inhabitants of the valley, her brothers Sol and Mose Garner. They were entranced with the pictures, invited me to eat with them, and they showed me how they "made" (i.e., grew or manufactured) everything they used except a little coffee and sugar which the brothers would buy on a rare hike or horseback ride into Sherwood. The road put in for logging was still in the future.

At one time, they told me, the Cove had a population of thirty or forty people, and there was an Episcopal mission church served by seminary students, one of sixteen or eighteen in the area around Sewanee. Had they ever been counted in the census? No.

A couple of years later I was talking to friends on the magazine section of the Nashville *Tennessean,* and a redoubtable team of journalists, alerting a census-taker, headed for Lost Cove. They did a fine feature, with pictures, and the Garners swelled the U. S. census of 1950 by precisely three.

Nashville *Tennessean* Magazine, 1950, and ABC, assorted notes.

SALE OF LOST COVE

T he credibility of the historian falls in a heap when he gets into the realm of the apocryphal story. Although the previous account of the Garners is documentable, the next undoubtedly has some embroidered edges. It is told because it is at least partly true—all of it could have happened, and certainly some of it did.

In the early thirties, news travelled slowly of the dramatic proposal to bring to the remote forests of the winding Tennessee River valley the greatest power and conservation project ever attempted by man on the planet. News, that is, travelled slowly in Tennessee. Readers of papers all over the country knew more about the proposed TVA than did the people whose lives would be so profoundly affected by it.

There were, as always, speculators seeking the fast buck, and such a group of four men appeared one day at the Garner cabin in Lost

Cove. Unknown to the non-literate farming family, the foreigners—from New York or Chattanooga or somewhere like that—had done their research well. They knew, for instance, that the government was committed to paying reasonable prices for all land, but that special consideration would be given all power producers or owners of dams and lakes, this a precaution to neutralize the power lobby.

Sophisticated engineers had spotted on a contour map the freak-of-nature called Lost Cove—a closed-in valley about six miles long, three miles wide, and potentially capable of impounding a lake 600 feet deep. Egress for the sixty inches of rainfall a year which could quickly make a body of water out of such a natural basin had been provided from time immemorial by Lost Cove Cave, draining the area from Slaughter Pen Hollow and Point Disappointment on down toward Crow Creek Valley. Furthermore the whole cove was owned by three people who couldn't read or write.

"We've come to bring you a great opportunity," said the slickers, as they unfolded their offer. In the spirit of philanthropy they would make it possible for this family, so remote from the world, to emerge from isolation with a princely sum of money—enough to buy all manner of wonderful Things. They could have a radio, a car, plumbing, electric lights, and all the wonders of the civilized world which had thus far been kept from them. It was all very easy. The engineers were prepared to offer in cash the sum of $18,000 for this inaccessible tract—one dollar an acre. Similar land in neighboring coves could be had, they said, for twenty cents an acre.

The Garners, whose Texas cousin John Nance had become Vice-President, caucussed. They came back speaking as one: "We don't want to sell." The strangers felt that perhaps the simple folk had not understood, so they went back, step-by-step, over the proposal and upped the purchase to $35,000. Another caucus and another refusal . . . and so on until the final take-it-or leave it proposition—$75,000! Somewhat to the surprise of the wrangle-weary quartet, the Garners said "OK, we will sell."

Deeds were drawn up, a bag full of cash delivered, and the two brothers crossed the mountain to register the sale and deposit the money in the bank at the county seat at Winchester.

Surveyors came in, followed by a wagon bringing mysterious boxes. Soon a great explosion was heard, and the speculators came to warn the Garners that they must leave their cabin. Water would soon begin rising.

"All right," said the Garners. "When we see the water coming up, we will leave." The anxious visitors watched as the water, with its entrance to the cave blocked by the collapsed limestone, rose slowly. One foot, two feet—then no more. Investigation revealed that it was flowing into a new cave entrance a few yards away. Frantically another blast and another brought grim truth. The Saddle was honeycombed with caves.

Back to the Garners went the Northerners. They had thought this whole thing over and had changed their minds. They were prepared to make an offer of truly sacrificial nature. They would now sell the property back to the family for a bargain price—$70,000. The Garners hadn't even moved out of their home, and they would have a profit of $5,000.

There was a conference, and the brothers, speaking for themselves and their sister, said simply that they didn't want to buy the land.

What? Surely they hadn't heard aright. Surely they wanted this splendid tract which had such sentimental value—their family home for nearly a century. Nope. Sorry. "We just don't want it."

The bargaining began in reverse with the owners gradually coming down on their price. Finally, with salty tears, a last desperate offer was made. The owners would sell their recent acquisition for $18,000. The Garners talked it over and decided to buy.

Deeds were recorded, money exchanged, and the strangers returned, presumably whence they came.

ABC, notes from oral tales, cross-checked with county records, 1948-55. *Mose and Mucidore Garner died in 1952; Sol survived until August, 1957. Mose Garner had 144 heirs.*

NAMES

THE NAME Mucidore (spelled Mu-c-dore by its owner) long puzzled me. It had no relationship that I could perceive to the long list of colorful names of the region which go back to early England—

Servis Berry pronounced "Sarvis"; Gudger, a shortened variant of Goodyear.

At Tulane graduate school in 1951, I encountered a Franklin County schoolmate, Dr. Dick Taylor '32 named, like his ancestor the Confederate General, Dick and not Richard. He had married the brilliant Elizabethan scholar, Ailene McKenzie, from the Newcomb faculty. She knew precisely where the name came from. The hero of an obscure pre-Shakespearean play was Mucidorus. His name had reappeared in feminine form four hundred years later in lower Appalachia.

ABC from assorted notes, 1951-52. *Some place names include Tickbush, Bobtown (named after Robert E. Stewman, 1865-1899), Thumping Dick Hollow, Point Disappointment, Shakerag Hollow, Ragnation, Hat Rock, Jumpoff, Owl Hollow, Morgan's Steep, Fiery Gizzard, Tantalon, Slaughter Pen Creek, Bucket-of-Blood Cave, Cooley's Rift, Lost Cove Cave, and Crow Creek.*

THE QUESTION OF PROGRESS

Eva Lee Glass Appleby, on the porch at Rebel's Rest and apropos of the then-recent past, said to Professor Abbott C. Martin, "Everything is going to the dogs." When he agreed, she added, "I hope there won't be any more improvements."

Abbott Cotten Martin to ABC, August 11, 1952.

IMPROVEMENTS
(NOT ALL BAD)

In 1949, when the author was president of the Sewanee Civic Association, he appointed a committee for Long Range Planning, which set up three sub-committees to work for (1) an airstrip, (2) a lake, and (3) a highway cutoff to keep semi-trailers from passing through the campus when there were at that time 2,000 student-pedestrian crossings each day. Wendell Kline chaired the first committee, and in due

47

course (after enormous effort and ingenuity) there was a 2,800-foot, asphalt, lighted, beacon-protected strip with a lounge for pilots and a hangar for planes. As for the lake, Charles Cheston—almost over the bodies of those who said it couldn't be done—conjured up the first of more than a dozen, one of them happily named for him. The highway cutoff was a dreadful problem. Four successive governors promised, but the one who delivered—Gordon Browning—was the one against whom Sewanee had voted. The late Gaston Bruton could embellish accounts of the trips he and I made to the Capitol.

ABC, notes and recollections.

UPDATE

I F Miss SADA returned to Sewanee today, what would she recognize? Saints' Rest is no longer inhabited by Elliotts, but they live next door in the little house, and an Elliott is Dean of the College. Two of Kendal's cottages survive, while Greens live across the street. Fairbankses moved to the Curlycue Road a dozen years ago, and Rebel's Rest is the University's guest house. The Gorgases went to Tuscaloosa a hundred years ago, but the Hodgsons who bought the house maintain it in splendor and have provided four recent graduates. Miss Gibson's house was rescued by the Frank Thomases and is very handsome in its blue paint.

The professors are still wearing gowns as the trustees directed them to in 1869, but gowns for students were not adopted until six weeks after Miss Sada wrote her letter.

ENC, summer 1978.

CHAPTER THREE

PROFESSORS

RENOWN

A TTRACTED TO Sewanee in its early days were some remarkable men. One thinks immediately of a four-star general teaching mathematics (Kirby-Smith), Lee's chief of ordnance teaching engineering (Gorgas), a brigadier teaching metaphysics (Shoup), and the chaplain who missed election as Bishop of South Carolina narrowly (DuBose), but there were others less well known. For instance, John D. Phelan, who ran the first Inn, was a former supreme court justice in Alabama. A treasurer of the University, Samuel Goode Jones, built a railroad and had a town—Jonesboro, Georgia—named for him. Some think it was named for his son, who became governor, but that is wrong.

No tabulation of famous residents should omit the eight bishops who are buried in the cemetery—the largest collection in the country. There are Quintard and Gailor of Tennessee, Elliott of West Texas, Morris '89 of Panama and Louisiana, Carruthers '21 of South Carolina, Mitchell '08 of Arkansas, Juhan '11 of Florida, and Wyatt-Brown '05 of Harrisburg.

ABC, Miscellaneous notes.

DIGNITY

P ROFESSORS ALWAYS called the boys "Mister." It had a good effect on morale. It dignified them.

J. H. Johnston '87 to ABC, August 25, 1952.

PRESIDENT, C.S.A.

In the Sewanee Archives is the typescript of a reply from Jefferson Davis to Josiah Gorgas, headmaster of the Junior Department. Its rather obscure wording led Hudson Strode, Davis's biographer, to believe that the Confederate President was offered the Vice-Chancellorship of the University of the South, a post which General Gorgas accepted two years later. Quintard, the incumbent VC, was trying to resign to devote full time to his diocese. Davis mentions "home education" for his sons and his desire to be near them, which would exclude the theory that Gorgas had simply been encouraging him to become a trustee or a member of the executive committee. Gorgas's letter has not been found, and there is no reference to the matter in the *Proceedings*.

"J. D." to Gen. Josiah Gorgas, January 6, 1870, Sewanee Archives. *My guess is that Gorgas was trying to persuade Davis to move to Sewanee to live.*

NEAR-MISS

Early in Sewanee's first decade, when Jefferson Davis had been released from prison and hounding of him had abated, there was a good bit of communication between him and Sewanee. His daughter Winnie visited Dr. and Mrs. Henry M. Anderson, he the University Treasurer. The Andersons were kin to Mrs. Quintard, *née* Catherine Hand. Ex-president Davis addressed the board of trustees in 1872, offering to lead a campaign on behalf of the University by soliciting insurance buyers who would name the University beneficiary. The firm he headed would write the policies.

Proceedings, 1872. Today it seems a sad reflection on the judgment of the board that his offer was not accepted.

NO ORDINARY SET

T ODAY . . . completes my first week at the University. . . . We have concocted an Advent appeal to be sent to all the churches. I have written my first sermon for the boys. I spend several hours every day at my buildings [Magnolia, Palmetto and The Rectory on St. Augustine's Avenue] which are progressing favorably—and for which my arrival with the money and my presence were both opportune. I have relieved General Shoup of the morning and evening prayers. Mrs. [Josiah] Gorgas is very kind and takes admirable care of me. She got into my satchel and emptied it of the remains of my lunch—two partridges, etc.—which I had clean forgot. We have been to see so far the Elliotts, the Greggs, and the Greens [all bishops' families—ed.]. On night before last I attended the regular meeting of the E.Q.B. Club composed of professors and others, about a dozen in all, and I was very forcibly struck anew with the composition of the University. It was no ordinary set of men. After the literary entertainment which lasted until about 10 o.c. came the "Fecitiae"—an elegant supper which called out all the wit and humor of the company. This is once every two weeks, and is kept up with interest and spirit. I will write to Susie next. Kiss May and Haskell.

William Porcher DuBose to his wife Nannie Peronneau DuBose, November 25 and 27, 1871. *Slightly condensed.*

GREAT TEACHER

Y OU ASK me to be personal about what I have to say of Dr. DuBose. I did not have the advantage of sitting under him for three years but only for about three months. However, this converted me to his discipleship. . . . He opened the New Testament for me and through the New the Old. I owe to the Doctor not merely an explanation of the great doctrines of Christianity but a veritable philosophy of Christianity by which one can read the Holy Scriptures with understanding. His writings are my best commentary on all the Scriptures. Yes, he has been by far my principal teacher in things pertaining to God.

Bishop Albert S. Thomas '98 to ABC, November 27, 1956.

ALAS NO LASS

ONE DAY Dean DuBose was prevented from attending classes and he left a notice on the blackboard as follows:

Dr. DuBose will not meet classes today.

It being dance weekend, an enterprising student struck out letters as follows:

Dr. DuBose will meet lasses today.

The dean himself drifted back to the room, saw the student's handiwork, and rearranged the wording as follows:

Dr. DuBose will not meet asses today.

DeVane K. Jones to ABC, February 10, 1960.

COMPATIBLE

"DR. McCRADY drew illustrations freely from the physical and natural sciences, mathematics, psychology, ontology, philology, ethnology, mythology—all nature, all books, the Book. . . . Ten years ago on my way here I called on Prof. McCrady (in Charleston) and we talked of this place and its mission. . . . McCrady and this place were made for each other."

From funeral address by Chaplain William Porcher DuBose, *Cap and Gown,* October, 1881.

INTERIM VICE-CHANCELLOR

IN THE 1878-79 interim between the resignation of General Josiah Gorgas and the election of the Rev. Telfair Hodgson (1879-90) both John B. Elliott and General E. Kirby Smith (no hyphen yet) signed University documents as "Acting Vice Chancellor." Actually, the Hebdomadal Board was in charge.

Several letters, including promissory notes, in Archives.

JOHN McCRADY'S DIARY

O NE OF the three or four most interesting documents in Sewanee history is the Diary of John McCrady. With greatest frankness that learned man recorded little stories as well as big ones. At different times he had arguments with nearly all his colleagues, but he never lost their admiration. The spat with Quintard, recorded with some heat in both their diaries, is a good example.

McCrady's coming to Sewanee in 1877 from Harvard was perhaps the most important academic acquisition of the University's first two decades. According to Samuel Eliot Morison in *The Development of Harvard University*, Louis Agassiz, shortly before his death in 1873, brought from the College of Charleston his favorite student John Mc-Crady to take charge of instruction in zoology. Agassiz wanted to develop the graduate work then frowned on by President Charles Eliot. McCrady's first four candidates for the doctoral degree were William K. Brooks, who went to Johns Hopkins, Edward A. Birge, who became president of the University of Wisconsin, J. W. Fewkes, who became Chief of the Bureau of Ethnology in Washington, and Walter Faxon, who became McCrady's successor in zoology at Harvard. McCrady's resignation came when Eliot told him to concentrate on undergraduate teaching, which is not what he thought he had come to Harvard to do. The handsomest of Sewanee dormitories, designed by Edwin A. Keeble '23 of Nashville, is named for John McCrady and his family.

J ULY 15, 1878: This morning Mr. Van Hoose called to inform me that he had received telegrams from Cowan that Gov. Wade Hampton was on his way to the village on horseback, and to inquire from Gen. Gorgas whether I knew anything about his visit. Of course I was as ignorant as anybody—but went out with Mr. Van Hoose, and met Major Fairbanks and the Vice-Chancellor. The latter told us immediately that Mrs. Gorgas had divined the solution of the wonder by remembering that young Wade Hampton is courting Miss Percy—a young lady who has recently arrived here, sent it is said by her parents who wish her to marry young Sessums, whom she once refused, but who now graduates as first honor man. Even after this, the reports of Gov. Hampton's approach continued to come in—so that at last he was actually announced at the hotel. We sent to see who it was—and found that as Mrs. Gorgas supposed it was young Wade. The students called on him—and this afternoon I went there to leave a card, but he had already called on his lady love, and gone on to Beersheba Springs.

"Young Sessums" ('76) became the first Sewanee alumnus to be elected bishop (Louisiana). He married the daughter of Bishop Galleher and not Miss Percy.

August 24, 1878: This afternoon, General Smith invited both Posie and Edward to accompany us to the Natural Bridge, which is a far more picturesque and even beautiful spot than I imagined. Mr. Tomlinson lives close by. The pond is nothing but the pool made by the large spring.

September 8, 1878: Edward begged me to take a walk with him, and we went together to Green's View. It was a lovely sight with the great shadows of massive cumulus clouds, lying motionless on the mountain flanks and across the plain, while brilliant sunshine intensely illuminated every object between.

December 24, 1878: Our new serving man Green came today. He engaged at $6 a month for the winter. Wages to be raised in spring to $8 if he plants the garden.

INDEPENDENCE DAY

*F*ounders' *Day at Sewanee has been a movable feast. The true anniversary of the founding, July 4, when the Board of Trustees first met, came to be considered unsuitable. September 18, commemorating the opening of the institution in 1868, was celebrated for years until it came too close to the opening of the academic year to allow proper preparation. Finally Founders' Day settled in upon October 10, the anniversary of the 1860 laying of the cornerstone, perhaps the least significant of the three dates in the history of the University. Two versions of an early Fourth of July observance have survived.*

After rising late this morning and while dressing I heard a loud sound of the choir singing as if marching through the College grounds and before long Sallie came in and told me that Bp. Quintard had induced Dr. DuBose and the Chancellor to consent to a celebrational service of the day. I had not received the slightest intimations of it and Edward had been allowed to go as usual with the choir. I proceeded at once before breakfast to the Church and passing through Dr. DuBose's lecture room into the choir, sent the choir Proctor to call Edward out. . . . I made Edward disrobe and brought him home. My reasons were two: 1st because they had no right to force the boys into a celebration of this day without the consent of their parents, and 2nd because they had no right to implicate the Church in a political celebration; thus using it as a political engine. I heard that Bp. Quintard has voiced his belief that the only hope of the University is in "naturalizing" it, so that he can get money from the Northern churches.

John McCrady Diary, July 4, 1878.

HOSTILITIES

Last year, while services in recognition of the national holyday were being conducted in the Chapel, he [McCrady] came in and removed his little boy from the Choir, and told me afterwards that no son of his should be permitted to take part in any such service. This year, by his influence, there were no services in the Chapel on the 4th of July. . . . He does not seem to recognize that the war is over.

Charles Todd Quintard Diary, July 30, 1879.

SUPERFLUOUS ABILITY

"Prof. McCrady, the favorite pupil of the great Louis Agassiz, fills with almost superfluous ability, the chair of physics and biology, . . . As a lecturer he is most delightful, profoundly learned, yet clearly comprehensible. . . . He remains at Sewanee . . . for the reason that the others stay on, that they are held by the charm of the place, their friendly attachments to each other, and the consciousness of the highest duty worthily performed. . . ."

Unidentified clipping from New Orleans, datelined Sewanee, July 10, 1879. Loose in Charles Todd Quintard Diary.

DUELLING AT SEWANEE

Pᴇʀsᴏɴs ꜰɪɢʜᴛɪɴɢ a duel are advised to read the Ordinances of the University of the South.

> Established by the Board . . . with the provisions of the Amended Charter of Said University, granted by the Chancellor of the 4th District, on the 4th Monday of June, 1871, at Winchester. . . .
> Section 6. Be it further ordained: That any person who shall give, accept, or knowingly carry a challenge to fight a duel, or who shall publish or post another person as a coward, or use opprobrious language for not accepting a challenge, shall be fined not less than fifty dollars.

Proceedings of the Board of Trustees of the University of the South, 1871, p. 58, 59.

POST-BANNING OF POSTING

DuBose . . . says Col. Lovell [a resident of the community] has told Elliott that he considers it a breach of faith that Jaeger is permitted to remain here, and that he will proceed to post him [i.e., challenge him]. DuBose told Elliott to say that if Col. L. posts Jaeger, he [DuBose] will post him. I told DuBose that I will take my stand with him equally in the whole matter, though of course I shall be the one challenged by Lovell—but that I am prepared for it. I do not well see how the difficulty is to be avoided and have long felt that I might have to be a martyr in the struggle for the abolition of duelling.

John McCrady Diary, April 10, 1878.

56

E.Q.B. POST-MORTEMS

MAY 9, 1878. At the E.Q.B. Gen. Smith gave us a condensed account of the great campaign in which he completely defeated not only Gen. Banks but the whole system of Federal operations against the Trans-Mississippi Department in 1864. It is manifest that the success was due to the perfection of his strategic arrangements, although of course if Gen. Taylor and Gen. Price had not done their parts well as they did—no arrangements could have succeeded.

November 21, 1878: At the E.Q.B. Club Gen. Smith gave us a very clear account of Bragg's disastrous failure as a general in the Kentucky campaign. He claims to have suggested that campaign to Gen. Beauregard and to have striven in vain to make Bragg understand it. He confirms the statement that Bragg defeated the enemy both at Perryville and Murfreesboro and then retreated. He lost his head from a sense of his responsibilities.

John McCrady Diary.

PUDDING

AT DINNER to-day—6 P.M.—[were present] all our English guests, Messrs. Bolling and Garwood of Texas, my wife, daughter, and son. After dinner Professor McCrady, Dr. Hodgson and General E. Kirby Smith came in for the evening. General Smith brewed a bowl of very *fascinating* punch. At dinner we had plum pudding all the way from old England, and the Englishmen fairly doated on it. It is their national dish and refuses to flourish out of England. A Frenchman will dress like an Englishman, swear like an Englishman, and get drunk like an Englishman, but if you would offend him forever, compell him to eat plum pudding.

Charles Todd Quintard Diary, Christmas, 1880.

KIRBY-SMITH'S REWARD

"I'LL HAVE a high seat in heaven," General Kirby-Smith said, "for teaching calculus to theologs."

Rev. C. B. K. Weed '95 to ABC, December 7, 1951.

MATHEMATICIAN ON PLANTS

THE FLORA of Sewanee constitute a connecting link between North and South. Forms characteristic of the Green Mountains and Adirondacks mingle with forms from the Gulf and Atlantic slopes, with occasional wanderers from the trans-Mississippi. Southern types of leguminosae, northern and western compositae, delicate polygalas, and showy gerardias, hypericums, euphorbias, aenotheras, graceful bluets, and humble hepaticae, meet on this common borderground, and claim fellowship for every section of this great republic.

Written by General Edmund Kirby-Smith and quoted by David Haskins in 1877.

GENERAL ON ANIMALS

GENERAL KIRBY-SMITH's love for plants was equalled by his love for animals. Once in a discussion with Caleb Weed, who spent the winter of '92 with him, the General recollected his own cruellest action. It occurred during his service in the Mexican War. Walking through a field, he had noticed a lovely sprig of Calmia, and stopped to examine it. He collected a few branches and laid them on the ground while he examined other specimens nearby. When he started to pick up the branches, he found underneath them two rattlesnakes, coiled. He leaped back and quickly dispatched the snakes. Weed, puzzled, inquired how he happened to regard that as cruelty. "Well," replied the General, "they had a chance to kill me, and they didn't."

Rev. C. B. K. Weed '95 to ABC, December 7, 1951.

LETTER FROM SEWANEE

My Dear Fanny,

I am writing again, by proxy, for your mother. Her numerous cares take up so much of her time that she can not indulge much in her great fondness for writing. Our household is large, though it has not quite yet reached its normal summer growth. We have eleven boy boarders, two visitors, Mary DeMoville & Mrs. Clark. Lydia & Nina came today. Carry and Queeny will arrive tomorrow & Betty Selden is expected the 18th as also Mrs. Higgins, a permanent boarder (in our room) coming from Texas. I wish you could be here tomorrow. The great Vanderbilt Base Ball Match is to be played—a professional coach has been employed for the past two weeks, and excitement is running almost at fever heat—a large special train with ladies, gentlemen & students comes tomorrow from Nashville. [Sewanee won 11-3.]

Thursday we had a general parading and jubilee over the Historical Society which held its meeting here. I send you a paper in which it is largely reported. Sewanee is fast budding into general notice. Reporters are constantly visiting us & applications for building lots increase. Several new & pretty houses are going up. The Galleher building [Johnson Hall site] next door, being erected by Mr. Barker, is a pretty structure. Mrs. Haden is putting up a nice house. The Glass building will soon be completed. The foundations of the Gymnasium [later Convocation Hall] are about up and the corner stone will be formally & ceremoniously laid in a few days. Mr. Gailor's and Colonel Jones' houses are about completed. The poor Sigmas [SAEs] have not yet begun their building, their impecuniosity is the stumbling block. One of our boys Fant ['90] left for home, today, but Bohn ['88] takes his place. Speaking of building, you know your mother has built two wash-houses and rented them both. I suppose she will have to build a third to have her washing done at home. Lydia took the first honors—both the girls look well. Bepy has grown very much, she is even taller than Lydia—the three girls are bright & attractive beauties they say. You and Carry have neglected your advantages & must now step aside & let their attractions come into the limelight. Your Mother & I issue orders accordingly. You will have to stop also at Salem. I wish I could help you to enjoy the fish & crab of Norfolk. I do long for a sniff of the sea. The sound of the breakers was my lullaby as a baby, but the

59

coast with its fish & oysters & innumerable attractions gets farther off the older I grow. . . . The Gallehers have arrived, excepting the Bishop. The house is going up rapidly. I hope we shall see you soon, with love to all

Your af' father

Gen. E. Kirby-Smith to his daughter Frances [Wade], May 11, 1886.

STATUE OF THE GENERAL

My dear Frances:

The statue of Father in Washington was made by a sculptor C. Adrian Pillars of St. Augustine, Florida, 1913-1916. [It] was placed . . . through an act of the Florida legislature. Each state was allowed to place statues of two illustrious citizens. The first bill . . . passed in 1906, was introduced by John Beard from Escambia County [but] did not carry an appropriation. . . .

Four years later, when I opened my office to practice medicine in Jacksonville, nothing had been done. . . . With a great deal of time, expense, and politics, I had another bill introduced . . . in 1913 with an appropriation of $10,000. . . . The three commissioners appointed by the governor (old Confederate veterans) took about two years. . . . I think they spent $3,500 on themselves as Mr. Pillars only received $6,500. . . . As far as I know this is the only statue of Father. . . . We have in one of our central parks a monument to Confederate heroes. On the base there is . . . the inscription "E. Kirby-Smith, a Christian soldier." . . .

Yours affectionately,
Lee

Dr. J. Lee Kirby-Smith '93 to his sister Frances Wade, March 5, 1934. *This is the only statue of a Sewanee faculty member in the national Capitol building. Alumnus William Crawford Gorgas '75 is in New York University's Hall of Fame.*

RELIEF

O N OCCASION General Kirby-Smith would tease students. Dr. Oscar Torian remembered coming into the General's office as a freshman, and he found the General pretending to be very tough. The General said, "Who sent you?" and Oscar replied, "The Schedule Committee." The General let forth a blast, "What do they mean, sending me another student when they know all of my classes are already full?" etc., etc. And then as young Torian was beating a hasty retreat, the General kindly said, "Oh, come on back, I'll sign it."

Dr. Oscar N. Torian '96 to ABC, December 1, 1951.

INFLUENCE

T o GENERAL KIRBY-SMITH each student presented a limitless opportunity. One of his students, the son of a wealthy Texan, was well-named Tom Crank ['96]. The shiftless youngster would not study math. When time came to go home for the winter vacation, his father arranged for him to stay at General Kirby-Smith's for private tutoring. One evening the General came into the living room at Powhatan and gave Crank an audible bawling out. "I'm worried," he later told an older student. "I am afraid I've lost my influence with that boy."

Rev. C. B. K. Weed '95 to ABC, December 7, 1951.

ACCOLADE

O NE OF the students who became chief engineer of the Western Pacific Railroad told me some years ago that he owed all he was as an engineer to his four years under Kirby-Smith and all he was as a man to the fact that he spent those years at Sewanee.

Thomas Frank Gailor, unpublished MS in Archives, "The Faculty in 1882," p. 60.

SILVER STANDARD

T HE SILVER wedding anniversary of General and Mrs. Kirby-Smith—September 25, 1886—was a great event. Guests came from far and near, and the gifts were numerous. I remember one particularly from an old student. When "Mother Dear" opened the package and read the card she said, "Oh, if R— had only sent me something on his back board bill instead of these after-dinner coffee spoons—but they are handsome."

A T THE reception, a guest mentioned the eleven children (none married then), and the General's reply was, "I would be willing to go over all those years (he referred to the Mexican and Civil Wars) if God would give me eleven more children such as I've had." Mrs. K-S did not laugh with the others.

Queenie Woods Washington to ABC, November 14, 1951.

BOUNCING BETTYS

R ETURNING TO Powhatan from a dance one night, I was startled to see General Kirby-Smith in a long red flannel night shirt with a tennis racquet in his hand—hopping, jumping, striking wildly at something, I could not see what. It proved to be a bat. Sewanee was infested with bats and bouncing bettys before the days of screens. The General wore those night shirts summer and winter.

Queenie Woods Washington to ABC, November 14, 1951.

FEAR

I ASKED General K-S once if he was ever frightened in battle. His reply was "Hellfire and damnation, of course I was frightened—until I saw my brother killed before my eyes (in the Mexican War), and then I never felt a qualm of fear again."

Queenie Woods Washington to ABC, November 14, 1951.

SCHOONER

O NE OF the unforgettable moments in the life of Jack Shaffer occurred in Winchester at Davis's Bar when he saw the elegant and formidable "Miss Cassie" (Mrs. General) Kirby-Smith, order a schooner of beer, blow the top off, and quaff it like Falstaff.

J. Jackson Shaffer to ABC. August 19, 1952. *Dr. Rennie admits his mother liked an occasional beer but doubts that she ever drank it in a public place.*

FLORAL TRIBUTE

G ENERAL CHEATHAM was baptized, confirmed, married and buried by Bishop Quintard. The General was a much-loved cousin of my mother's and was often in our home for midday dinner. One day he said, "I must get away early, Marina, for the decoration at the cemetery." She said, "Oh, no, Frank. This is not Decoration Day." He replied, "No, but it is for the Yanks. I did all I could to kill them, and I'm willing now to put a flower on their graves."

Queenie Woods Washington to ABC, November 14, 1951. *Marina was also Miss Queenie's baptismal name.*

OUTDOOR ADVERTISING

A PATIENT FROM a nearby cove came to Emerald-Hodgson Hospital not long after Dr. Henry T. Kirby-Smith '27 had succeeded his father as chief of staff. "Dr. Smith," said the farmer, ignoring the hyphen as did most of the mountain people, "I didn't think I was gonna find you until I seen your sign on the highway." This momentarily puzzled Henry until he remembered the Kirby-Smith monument placed by the United Daughters of the Confederacy to obscure the Sigma Nu house. Henry replied, "Oh, *that* sign. It's not mine. It's grandpaw's."

Mary Phillips Woolverton Kirby-Smith to ABC, about 1955.

MEDICAL MANNERS

In some aspects the medical school was out of step with the rest of the University community. Many of the "meds" were not of the same social and economic background as the other students. They were sometimes not even high school graduates. The consequent disparity in decorum was encouraged, if anything, by strong-minded Dean John S. Cain, whose behavior at Commencements could be less than that high standard of formality so dear to the hearts of many Sewaneeans. When Dr. Cain presented her nursing diploma to Miss Bessie Octavia Brougher in 1906, he told her and the congregation in St. Augustine's Chapel, "A nurse must have the wisdom of Socrates and the strength of Samson. She must be able to turn over the largest patient like a Mississippian flips a flapjack." The students laughed. The matrons were less amused.

ABC, from undated notes.

OUT OF THE KNIGHT

Bishop Knight's term as VC (1914-1922) came at a most difficult time. The University was still reeling from its near-collapse in 1909 when five departments closed—medicine, law, nursing, dentistry, and engineering. World War I intervened and Sewanee made a slow recovery. However, the Bishop made at least three significant contributions to the University: he paid off an accumulated debt of $300,000, he launched and substantially completed a drive for $1,000,000; and he greatly improved the physical plant. It was he who thought of using the weathered field stone, both cheaper and more beautiful than the squared blocks of sandstone used in earlier construction.

David A. Shepherd '00 to ABC, June 3, 1952. *Ralph Peters Black '00 also claimed complicity in "discovering" pick-up stone. Take your choice.*

64

STILL KNIGHT

For a number of years, during and after the administration of Bishop Albion W. Knight as Vice-Chancellor, it was fashionable to criticize him for alleged inadequacies. To set the record straight, here is a tabulation of some of the accomplishments of his eight-year term—which included the dislocations of World War I.

Buildings erected or begun:

Cloister between Convocation Hall and Walsh; Cannon Hall; Sewanee Inn (now Elliott Hall); Quintard Hall rebuilt after fire; new Hoffman; Ormond Simkins Field House; six stone houses for faculty; Emery Annex to Hospital; Magnolia Dining Hall remodeled; Thompson Union remodeled; four homes given by the Benedicts.

Other items:

Golf links begun; electric power brought to Mountain; Dixie Highway brought through campus; University lands re-surveyed; sewer system started and water system expanded; debt of $300,000 cleared to qualify for gifts from General Education Board and Carnegie; approximately $1,000,000 raised.

Excerpted from Sarah H. Torian to Edward McCrady, October 13, 1954.

GOOD HOUSEKEEPING

Dr. John Nottingham Ware, professor of French, rushed over to help while the Bishop Knight home burned. He heard someone say there were valuable papers in the attic. Resourcefully, and at great danger to life and limb, he made his way to the master bedroom where was located the trap door to the attic. With no ladder the case appeared hopeless when he bethought himself of the idea of bouncing on the bed, trampoline style. He had made a couple of good jumps when through the window came Mrs. Knight's voice calling, "John Ware, get your dirty feet off my bed."

Dr. John N. Ware to ABC, about 1950.

LITTLE THEATRE

I NSTITUTIONS-WITHIN-INSTITUTIONS sometimes get lost. During the Depression of the thirties, when Spartan penury pervaded Sewanee, Major MacKellar '90 (the only stone-deaf professor of public speaking in America) wanted a Little Theatre. Upstairs in old Thompson Union was a movie theatre operated at considerable profit by the redoubtable and resourceful Tony Griswold '28. To prevent Professor MacKellar's student dramatics from encroaching on his audience-count, Griswold found devious means of raising money for a "theatre" (seating at most forty people) on the first floor. To guard himself from attack by the most powerful orator on the local scene, he dubbed it "The MacKellar Little Theatre" and sailed through the next decade with only occasional interruptions of his film schedule.

John Hodges '34 and others to ABC, March 1, 1956, *et seq.*

WHERE THERE'S SMOKE

T HE SEDLEY WARES lived where Cannon Hall now stands. Mary was a youngster when she woke up one night and called her father, saying, "I smell smoke." "No, you don't," he said, "go back to sleep." A little later she said, "Dad, the smoke is in my eyes." "Nothing of the kind," he assured her. Finally she yelled, "Dad, the whole house is on fire," and bolted for a window, climbing down a tree. The house was a total loss. The Wares saved only their night clothes. Dr. Ware had to borrow class notes from students to put back together his lectures. A textbook completed and in typescript was lost, and he never attempted to do it over.

Queenie Woods Washington to ABC, November 22, 1951.

BLESSED

S. L. Ware and his mother had an audience with the Pope in Rome. Dr. Ware borrowed a suit from a waiter at the hotel. It was too big and Mrs. Ware pinned it at the waist. At the most inappropriate moment the pin came out and there was a flurry of confusion as Mrs. Ware and the doctor attempted to keep his pants from going to the floor while performing the routine curtsies. Afterward Mrs. Ware said, "Why I had him blessed by the Pope I'll never know, but I figured I had done everything else for him."

Ann Vinton to ABC, November 9, 1962. She had indeed. She financed his superb education and provided so handsomely from her income that the Doctor contributed his priceless professorial services to the University for the better part of his career.

SPACED OUT

THE REV. CARY BRECKINRIDGE WILMER, professor in the School of Theology, was forgetful. He also had a blind spot—remembering which time zone was which. When he moved to Sewanee from Atlanta, he solved that problem by wearing two watches, one set on Sewanee time and the other on Atlanta's. About his absentmindedness is told this possibly apocryphal story. He asked a parishioner, "How is your mother?" She replied, "Dr. Wilmer, you buried her yesterday."

Some unrecorded raconteur to ABC, about 1960.

ABSTEMIOSITY

DR. REYNOLD M. KIRBY-SMITH was an abstemious man, limiting himself to one barrel of whiskey a year which he customarily bought from Uncle Dunk Tate.

Frank Fortune (Senior) to ABC, October 14, 1955.

SOURCE

Because of his passion for accuracy, Dr. Reynold Kirby-Smith '95 was a treasured source for Sewanee anecdotes. When asked for his earliest memories of Sewanee, he recalled that he had gone through St. Luke's Hall when it was being built. It was finished in 1879, and he was born in 1875. He said his greatest childhood fright was when the McCrady house [Otey Hall near the Walsh Hall site] burned. He was seven then and wouldn't go near the fire but knelt in the hedge of the Galleher house [Johnson Hall site] to pray. When he was 79, Dr. Kirby-Smith said, "Old folks are too gregarious. I remember clearly what happened, but my contemporaries get things mixed up."

Dr. R. M. Kirby-Smith '95 to ABC, April 7, 1954.

DELAY

Dr. Reynold Kirby-Smith was just a little boy when I was at Sewanee. I believe he was the one who was trying to say his prayers one night while I was there as a paying guest. His sister began tickling his bare feet. He said, "Excuse me, Lord, wait a minute while I knock the stuffing out of this girl."

Mrs. D. P. Holland to ABC, February 2, 1953.

SYMPTOMS

When Mrs. Henry T. Soaper died, Dr. Oscar N. Torian '96 and Dr. Reynold M. Kirby-Smith '95 set out by train for Harrodsburg for the funeral of the wife of their old friend. The train out of Chattanooga was crowded, and Dr. Torian had to take an upper berth above Dr. Kirby-Smith. They had difficulty sleeping because of the rough roadbed through Kentucky mountains. They had to dress early in the morning, and Dr. Torian, then past seventy, had a difficult time with his feet in the arms of his undershirt. As he finally got his pants on, he heard low moans from below. "For God's sake, Oscar, come help me. My feet have swelled up. I can't get my shoes on. It must be that whiskey I drank last night. I can't see very good either." Dr. Torian tumbled barefooted to the aisle of the Pullman and felt for the Kirby-Smith pulse. They concluded they might be witnessing advance symptoms of a heart attack. Together they got Dr. K-S dressed, having a terrible time with the shoes which were indeed very tight. Dr. Torian finished dressing and put on his own shoes to find that *his* feet had shrunk. By then it was light enough to see that they had switched shoes. The heart attack was warded off.

Herbert E. Smith '03 to ABC, February 26, 1954.

CONTRACT

Dᴇᴀɴ Hᴜɢᴇʀ W. Jᴇʀᴠᴇʏ '00 at times taught night classes in the law school at Columbia University. Once there was a taxicab strike with which Jervey was in sympathy. The strike was occasionally being broken by "scab" drivers. Jervey, in a hurry, signaled a taxi across the street. When it whirled around to pick him up, he saw that it was a scab cab. He backed off, thinking he should decline the ride. The driver recognized him and said, "Dr. Jervey, I studied law in your night class. When you waved your hand you made a contract. If you don't ride with me, you will have to pay for the ride." Jervey got in.

Ewing Y. Mitchell '33 to ABC, June 10, 1965.

MONEY TALKS

Iꜰ ᴏɴᴇ counts a student generation as four years, the immortal "Knickie" alternately panicked and gadflied a half dozen generations. William Skinkle Knickerbocker, editor of the *Sewanee Review* longer than anybody else, also taught a full load as head of the English department and had time to pop into and out of nearly every controversy in sight.

On one occasion his Shakespeare class was drowsing. Without changing the tone or tempo of his lecture he removed from his pocket a dollar bill. Slowly, talking right on, he tore it in half, then in quarters, and finally into tiny pieces, walked to the Walsh Hall window overlooking the quadrangle and threw the pieces out. By then everyone was wide awake, and not a syllable was missed the rest of the period.

John B. Ransom '42 to ABC, February 26, 1972.

PATRIOTIC

SHORTLY AFTER the Knickerbockers arrived at Sewanee in 1926, Mrs. K. was made welcome by the local chapter of the UDC. She went to a meeting or two at which all talk centered around plans for entertaining the national convention, being held for the first time at Sewanee. To honor the newly-arrived family it was suggested that son Charles '43, then five, might march in the parade and carry a Confederate flag. Since the youngster's two great-grandfathers had died for the Union, Professor K. made a counter offer. Charles could march if he could carry the Confederate flag on one shoulder and the American flag on the other. The offer was rejected.

Dr. William S. Knickerbocker to ABC, January 18, 1966.

The atmosphere had changed sufficiently by 1942 that student Dominic Ciannella managed, without injury, to walk out on the Choir when the Confederate flag was carried in the procession.

Very Rev. David B. Collins '43 to ABC, August 1, 1962.

70

BONNIE BEVAN

THE REV. DR. WILSON LLOYD BEVAN, professor at St. Luke's in the twenties and thirties, was extremely learned and extremely unorganized in his lecture methods. On many occasions he would stop in the middle of a sentence and send a student to the library. Bishop Jones recalled one such incident. "Jones, go down the hall and get me a volume of Hastings' *Encyclopedia of Religion and Ethics*." Jones inquired, "Which volume, Dr. Bevan?" The professor replied, "Oh, any volume. There's something in all of them that we don't know." Then he would let the book fall open anywhere, pick a citation almost at random, and for the rest of the period regale the class with a detailed discussion of the background of the article, or the life of the author, or both.

Dr. Bevan, despite his prodigious memory, could not recall faces. On one occasion Bishop Jones and a fellow student, the future bishop Charles James Kinsolving, decided to cut a class of which they constituted two-thirds of the membership, the one-third being Elnathan Tartt. They strolled to the village for a cup of coffee at the Tiger and were returning when they ran squarely into Dr. Bevan. The good-natured teacher laughed and said, "Ah, so you cut class today. There was nobody there but Jones." Tartt was inconsolable when he learned that his fidelity had gone unrecognized.

Bishop Girault M. Jones '28 to ABC, August 29, 1971.

ABBO

ABBO MARTIN's full name was Abbott Cotten Martin. During the four decades that he needled his students at Sewanee, he loved and he hated. He loved the Confederacy, France, British nobility, kings, queens, bishops, rich people, Republicans, Robert E. Lee, segregation and bourbon whiskey. He hated Methodists, Yankees, and Germans, or so he alleged with the most vehement articulateness. It was anomalous that he should have become admired, respected, and perhaps even beloved by, of all people, Germans.

71

During World War II one of the sites selected for the minimum security incarceration of German prisoners was Tullahoma, Tennessee. The American commandant of the camp cast about for ways in which his charges could be usefully and healthfully employed. By chance the Vice-Chancellor of the University of the South was offered a contingent of prisoners to be delivered daily to the campus for whatever needed doing. One of Abbo's known weaknesses was his penchant for grubbing in gardens, and for this reason or some other he was asked if he could deal with a platoon of captive workers. His Old South bias thus challenged, Abbo's Alley was begun. Some of his Aryans could speak French, and he could smatter German, so that communication was more than a remote possibility. He had them chopping, clearing, selectively slashing, smoothing footpaths, building footbridges, and planting any flower which would grow in this latitude. All the while he harangued them in his pidgin German on the evils of rigidity, authoritarianism, Goethe, Wagner, Kaisers, and Hitlers, and the sublimity of Wordsworth, Coleridge, and Voltaire. Alexander Guerry had vast imagination, but I shall always deplore the fact that he did not award those guys A.M. degrees. They earned them.

Beside Abbott Cotten Martin, most professional Southerners could be rated as semi-professional bush-leaguers at best. In class he employed the Outrageous as a teaching instrument. In his mighty one-man campaigns against Methodists and Temperance, he told of secret passageways leading from Church Headquarters into the cellars of the capitol at Washington. Sometimes he was believed. Yankees were anathematized with regularity and variety. Attacked on one occasion for his pro-Southern posture, he said in stout denial, "I have no objection to the North. It is beautiful. I only despise the *people*. Even among them, however, I find it in my heart to forgive those who come South to learn better ways."

ABC, assorted notes and recollections.

PROPITIATORY PRACTICES

During World War II Abbo customarily spent short vacations in Memphis. He would go to Nashville and take the night Pullman. In those days he had the pleasant habit of taking a night cap. He asked the porter if he thought the conductor would object to his taking a drink. The porter said, "Why, no, the conductor will join you." Abbo went to the club car, found the conductor, asked his permission, and offered him some refreshment, which the conductor readily accepted. Over the drink, the conductor reminisced that Bishop Gailor often used the same sleeper between Nashville and Memphis and was the only person allowed to remain an extra hour on the car at either terminus. He did not like to shave while the train was moving. The conductor added, "When Bishop Gailor rode the sleeper 'Sewanee' he not only offered me a night cap, but also an eye opener."

Abbott C. Martin to ABC, February 26, 1958.

WHISKEY SAFE

Professor Martin had trouble with the key to his whiskey locker. One evening, in the days before he stopped drinking, Abbo came home after a hard afternoon in the Alley to find that his cabinet was locked and, horror of horrors, no key. With an axe he was able to prise open the door. He had no sooner poured a libation than he remembered where he had put the key. He resolved he would never allow himself to forget again. The next afternoon, however, he found the cabinet locked again and had no recollection whatever of the whereabouts of the key. This time the door resisted his axe, and in desperation he smashed open the cabinet. Hardly had he removed the slivered wood than he spotted the key—in plain view inside the broken chest.

Abbott C. Martin to ABC, September 27, 1958.

NO STONE UNTURNED

My dear Major,

Just a line to let you know that I have you constantly on my mind and am hoping that your recovery, and return to Sewanee, is not far off.

We are still without definite information as to whether we are to be included in the Army and Navy plan for the college. However, I believe our chances are good because of our splendid equipment and the vitality and energy of the Vice-Chancellor [Guerry] who has left no stone unturned in representing our interests. I am not yet convinced that the need for young man-power is so pressing as to necessitate the abolition of the liberal arts curriculum. I am more inclined to think that military necessity is the cloak behind which lurks the New Deal determination to gain control over all the educational agencies in the land, and that this is part and parcel of the New Deal intention to transform our democracy into some form of state socialism in the postwar period. . . . We all miss you here at Sewanee.

George M. Baker to Henry M. Gass, January 5, 1943. *GMB, may he rest in peace, remained a Republican till the end.*

USAF

W HEN IT was announced in 1951 that the University of the South would be assigned an Air Force unit—badly needed because of drafting for the Korean conflict—Dean George M. Baker said, "It is due to the effort, the persistence, the resourcefulness of Captain Wendell F. Kline (USN) that we are getting this Air Force ROTC unit."

George M. Baker to ABC. January 13, 1951. *On January 6 or 7, Vice-Chancellor Boylston Green, who had given up hope for getting the unit, telegraphed Kline from Washington, saying, "Cancel trip to Macon" (area headquarters for AFROTC). Kline had already left. Had he received the wire, Sewanee would not have had its two decades of happy experience with the Air Force officers' program.*

TUTORIAL

COMPOSURE AND COURTESY are illustrated in this story about Professor Tudor Seymour Long. A freshman just arrived was dimly aware of Sewanee's unusual traditions. He knew that there were proctors and gownsmen, but that was about all. Walking across the quadrangle with a sophomore, he heard "Hello, Professor," "Hello, Doctor," as they passed faculty members. The sophomore indicated an approaching figure and said, "That's your English teacher, Tudor Long." Our hero, thinking the first name a title, said "Good morning, Tutor." Mr. Long, concealing whatever surprise he felt, bowed gravely, acknowledged the greeting, and passed by.

Dr. John L. Tison '34 to ABC, about 1933. *Mr. Long is remembered by the "Tudor S. Long Memorial Walk" held every year from Chattanooga to Sewanee under the aegis of Professor Hugh Caldwell. The silver service given Mr. Long by the alumni upon his retirement in 1956 is regularly used preceding the monthly meetings of the College faculty in the Bishop's Common.*

TELEGRAPHY

ABOUT THE time Edward McCrady received his Ph.D. in biology at the University of Pennsylvania in 1933, he was approached by Vice-Chancellor Benjamin Finney '91 as a possible replacement for Professor Willy should that gentleman vacate the chair of biology. In 1937, the trustees instigated the ousting of Mr. Willy over Dr. Finney's objections, and Dr. McCrady was the logical choice. Dr. Finney would not issue the invitation on the ground that Willy should not have been fired. Accordingly the "invitation" came from the Chancellor, Bishop Theodore D. Bratton '82. It consisted of a telegram advising of the election. Dr. McCrady almost decided not to accept because of the unusual nature of the invitation. The same technique was employed a year later, again almost without success, in the election of Alexander Guerry '10 as Vice-Chancellor.

Dr. Edward McCrady to ABC, April 9, 1956.

LAUNDRY

Spanish Professor Timothy Pickering rushed to Chapel still a little fuzzy from grading midsemesters. Obviously not in need of a clean heart, he startled his neighbors by reading in a clear pious voice, "Give me a clean shirt, O Lord." His wife, Bun, was a mite resentful at the prayer, as she had just ironed a basketful, and doesn't know to this day what his unconscious was up to.

Mrs. A. T. Pickering to ABC, November 14, 1957.

BUSINESS PROMENADE

Vice-Chancellor Alexander Guerry was for all seasons. As an administrator, however, he was the best I ever knew—and that is quite a few. His originality and imagination were seasoned by his wife's astute critical judgment. I have seen Dr. Guerry walk across the quadrangle to the Supply Store and transact more business than a normal person would in a solid day. He had instant recall, on meeting anyone, of what he had been planning, possibly for days, to say to that person.

ABC, assorted recollections.

FAITHFUL SERVANT

You may make journeys to scores of American colleges and you may come away half puzzled and half impressed: You survey, you ponder, you sigh. Then you go to Sewanee and see what Alexander Guerry is doing. Alas, the tragedy is that you have to revise the tense of that verb: you go to Sewanee and see what Vice-Chancellor Guerry and like-minded men had done, until the dark instant when he died Tuesday in Knoxville of a heart attack. When you examine what that faithful servant and his devoted faculty had been undertaking at the University of the South, you might not agree with the

76

educational philosophy behind the program and the discipline, but you knew this: he and his associates believed in belief. They had confidence in the ideal of Christianity they applied, and because of their confidence they had cheer, calm, and freedom from the gnawing misgivings of institutional executives torn between two ideals. This did not make Sewanee monastic. Students would laugh aloud at any such suggestion. They had their fun, they enjoyed their golf course, they delighted in their simple fraternity houses, they would go off for the week-end and raise a good deal of cain in some instances. But they came back to the school with the conviction that after all it *was right*. When they sang in their chapel and looked up at the altar, there was in their eyes a light that all the dazzle or the darkness of afteryears could not destroy. Alexander Guerry did not create that spirit, he inherited it, he developed it, he exemplified it and made it so much a part of himself and of his home that it was pervasive. He welcomed to his home the students and their parents, and by his simple gentleness he did as much as by the exercise of his fine, discriminating mind. Usually when a Southern leader passes, one is tempted to ask, What made him what he was? How did he come to have that outlook on life? One does not feel that one is performing a moral autopsy when he tries to look into the heart of the average man. It is not so with Alexander Guerry. There was about him so much of spirituality that reverence restrains inquiry. You think of him as he walked among men. You remember how he labored for Sewanee and for the cause of Christian education when he knew that every beat of his impaired heart might be the last. You recall conversation with him about the things that are eternal, and you have neither the wish nor the need to probe and cut and dissect. One sentence spoken by Him who sat by the well of Samaria explains Alexander Guerry and makes you stand in awe by his honored bier—"I have meat to eat that ye know not of."

Douglas Southall Freeman as reprinted from *The Richmond News Leader* in *Sewanee Alumni News*, August 1949.

CHAPTER FOUR

STUDENTS

CONFLAGRATION

MAJOR FAIRBANKS was the custodian of the boys' allowances, and there I went each month for my dollar with which to buy a bottle of lemon syrup or hair oil. The Major was a strict disciplinarian and his pet aversion was a boy with a grimey face or soiled collar. We wore paper collars in those days and sometimes a paper shirt-front to conceal one not so tidy.

Coming to Sewanee in 1869 as the only student from the North, I was surprised at the friendly greeting. Boys of Sewanee were of gentle birth and breeding and only once was I taunted with having come from the home of Abraham Lincoln.

Coming from Springfield to Sewanee, the railroads were in a dilapidated condition. The tracks were not ballasted, the cars creaked and groaned and shifted from side to side. They were built of wood, heated by a wood stove, and lighted by oil lamps. The trains were controlled by hand brakes. One toot on the whistle by the engineer meant put on brakes, and two toots meant let them go. When I went back home from Sewanee I took passage on a "floating palace" in Nashville, an old stern wheeler going down river to Cairo then by rail to Springfield.

My dormitory, Tremlett Hall, was occupied by students on the upper floor and by Col. T. Frank Sevier and General Josiah Gorgas on the first floor. On one occasion two boys were emptying a wooden tub of waste bathing water and it spilled through the loose floor boards into the General's apartment below. I do not remember what reward the boys got.

Down the ravine near Tremlett Spring was a small outhouse. One night coming back with a pail of water, I pushed a piece of paper under the shingles and set it afire. I realized the excitement would not be good for my hide so I put it out, or thought I did. Proceeding up the hill I was passed by boys rushing down with a cry of "fire." The boys turned the house bottom side up. The fire was put out. I escaped with a tongue-lashing from Col. Sevier.

Edited from letters, recollections of 1869, John S. Bradford '73 to ABC, 1947-48.

KISSES

Social usage at Sewanee in the eighties was much as it was elsewhere in the far-flung moral empire of Queen Victoria. Being engaged to a man, for instance, by no means meant that a girl could with propriety kiss him. Miss Queenie's sister, engaged for three years, kissed the groom-to-be for the first time on the night before her marriage. One day in 1887 Sewanee buzzed with the news that, on the previous evening, John Doggett '88, later Judge Doggett of Jacksonville, had kissed (without being engaged to) Kate Pritcherd in Nashville. Miss Queenie was sought out by the embarrassed Kate, protesting her innocence, and imploring help in deflecting the rumors. Miss Queenie earned her niche in Kate's demonology by saying with feigned horror, "I didn't think *he* would do that!"

Queenie Woods Washington to ABC, November 22, 1951.

WEDLOCK

Student Walter Barnwell '88 boarded with Mrs. John McCrady. One evening past midnight he appeared with a girl and announced that he was married. Mrs. McCrady promptly moved into action. She said to him, "You go into that room and stay there until I call you." She said to the girl, "You go to that other room and stay there." She sent for the Rev. Doctor DuBose and had him perform a marriage ceremony in her parlor. Then, but only then, she let them go to bed.

Chaplain Ellis M. Bearden '15 to ABC, January 20, 1961.

PREY PROCTORIAL

STUDENT PRANKS were just as lusty and just as imaginative in the late nineteenth century as in the mid-twentieth. For instance, there was tight-wiring. On a shadowy walk at night, fractious undergownsmen would stretch a wire between posts, trees, or stakes about six inches above the ground. A puddle in the path beyond was not considered a liability. So frequent became the incidence of the game in 1885 that the ultimate punishment—expulsion—was announced. In that year three friends could not resist a perfect setting. They stretched their wire and heard, nearing them on the walk, the voice of that most worthy prey, the head proctor, John Gass. They gasped with anticipation. But then—a girl's voice. A date was with him, dressed for the dance. Aghast, miserable, wilted—the three plotters were transfixed. At the last possible moment, one of them jumped the fence in front of the couple, saluted smartly, and said, "There is a wire in front of you, Mr. Gass." The grave proctor saluted in return and said, "Thank you, Mr. Green." The teller of the story concludes, "Paul's action has seemed to me to illustrate that indefinable 18-carat something that Sewanee always adds."

E. L. Wells, Jr. '89 to ABC, October 24, 1953.

MASTER CHARGE

HENRY HOSKINS, who operated the garage and hack at the turn of the century, met Brinkley Snowden getting off the train after a lapse of years. Hoskins greeted him pleasantly and said, "You owe me $1.30." Snowden gladly paid it, but asked why Hoskins had not written him a note about it. The hack driver said, "Oh, I knew I would see you some time."

J. Bayard Snowden '03 to ABC, September 10, 1956.

STUDENT AID

S TUDENT BEN FINNEY '91 of Virginia had to leave school because he was broke. Sewanee's fortunes too were at a low ebb. The faculty had been asked again to accept scaled wages. Finney had hardly arrived home when he received a letter from a group of his professors telling him that they had made up a purse to pay his tuition. He could take turns living with them if he would return. He did, and when he became Vice-Chancellor (1922-38) he never forgot the point-of-view of the poor student. His wealthy wife died before he became VC and left her fortune to their son, whose memoirs of his life among the movie set are worth reading.

David A. Shepherd '00 to ABC, November 18, 1951, and interviews with Ben Jr. at New York's 21 Club.

DEMON RUM

D RINKING AT Sewanee reflected the mores of Episcopalians. The church itself placed no anathemas upon drinking. Drunkenness, however, was intolerable. It was bad manners, ungentlemanly. But social drinking has always been a part of the Sewanee scene among faculty members and usually among students, although rarely with propriety together until about 1960. In the Grammar School there were rigid rules against drinking, which were rather consistently enforced. Among the college students it was the policy to make intoxicants difficult to obtain and sometimes illegal to keep in dormitories. There was no legal drinking prior to World War II in fraternity houses, no drinking on the dance floor. No pledge of abstinence was required. Non-drinking was not a matter of the Honor Code, a fact which may account for the Honor Code's success. The drinking was done by men only, not the girls, and usually from a jug behind a tree. Most faculty members looked the other way unless the effects became obvious. Then a couple of students would take the celebrant to his room. Only under Vice-Chancellor Hodgson was there a determined effort to prohibit all drinking among all students. It failed.

Various sources, including Dr. R. M. Kirby-Smith '95 to ABC, October 10, 1954.

MANEUVERS

A GAME CALLED "Corners" was popular at Palmetto Hall before the turn of the century. Upperclassmen on the first floor would yell "Corners," and freshmen, who were quartered on the second floor, were expected to dash toward the walls. The fiends below would then playfully fire pistols through the center of the ceiling.

ABC, miscellaneous notes. *I deem this an old-timers' exaggeration. I can't believe it happened more than once or twice.*

BATTLE LINES

W HEN OLD Sewanee Inn was a grammar school dormitory, bedbugs infested the plaster walls and were enormous. At night they trooped forth like soldiers. The cadets tested their fencing finesse by trying to pin the varmints to the wall with bayonets. The idea was not so much an attempt to reduce the bedbug population as to compete in good clean indoor sport.

J. Jackson Shaffer '07 to ABC, *circa* 1948, on his porch in Louisiana.

This "old Sewanee Inn" was a white frame building on the site of Elliott Hall. Its wide porches may be seen in the 1910 projection of the central campus which includes a towerless All Saints' Chapel and Old Hoffman, athwart the present highway. The Grammar School moved to Quintard Hall in 1902.

POTTERY

T HE BOYS living in St. Luke's Hall in 1910 called the rooms "baseball suites" because the most important properties were a pitcher and a catcher, the latter being the thunder-mug which took the place of inside plumbing.

Bishop Frank A. Juhan '11 to ABC, December 15, 1958.

POKERS AND KNIVES

During the days when students went home in December to return in March there was no great need for furnace heat. In the brisk fall or early spring the boys kept warm before open grates. The first thing a newcomer would do would be to heat a poker and burn his name in the mantlepiece. The matron would reprove him, as ladies should. Frequently fraternity insignia, or girls' initials, would be added. Consternation was wrought, though, one year at Kendal. A new instructor refinished his mantlepiece, obliterating several decades of red-hot poker works. Miss Mamie Cotten was furious.

I noticed an inside door in my garage, probably removed from a junk heap by Mrs. MacKellar, a famous collector. There appeared a name, not burned but carved, H. R. Gaither [grammar school '04]. I surmised that it must have belonged to the father of the then president of the Ford Foundation. I took the whole door to Lester Finney who cut the carved piece out and polished it beautifully. On my next trip to New York I personally presented it to H. Rowan Gaither, Jr., regaling him with stories of his father's days at Sewanee. When the University presented to the Foundation in 1961 its successful request for $2½ million, the president had a reminder of the University of the South on his desk where it served as a paperweight.

ABC, assorted notes and recollections.

ARRIVING UNANNOUNCED

Johnny Clem '06 led a deputation from Shakerag Point to Aunt Lizzie Long's house to get some Mountain Dew. Miss Lizzie's father was seated in the yard. He had heard their approach and had a shotgun across his knee. He warned them against arriving unannounced and pointed toward a corner of his yard, saying, "There are two Revenuers buried there." Two revenue agents had indeed disappeared about a year previously, according to Clem.

Eric P. Cheape '10 to ABC, July 25, 1953. *Clem was the son of "the Drummer Boy of Shiloh" featured in a Walt Disney film.*

ASCENT

A RTHUR CROWNOVER '95 lived in Rowark's Cove near Wet Cave. During the years in which he was earning his bachelor's and law degrees, he walked up the Mountain to class. It was said that he tied the laces of his shoes together, slung them around his neck, and put them on when he got to the top. They lasted longer that way. Crownover became the first in a series of Sewanee graduates to go to the top in his field. He became presiding judge of the Tennessee Court of Appeals.

ABC, notes from the Archives.

JOURNALIST'S JOURNEY

T HOMAS EWING DABNEY, following his retirement as editor of a New Mexico newspaper, moved to Waveland, Mississippi. It was within bus-riding distance of Sewanee, and he came every summer to his boyhood home. For the last twenty years of his long life, he took a ritual walk—down the Mountain to Wet Cave, a thousand feet below. I went with him a couple of times and, although he was thirty years my senior, he was tough to follow. One story I remember, though I didn't write it down. When he graduated from Sewanee in 1905, he went to Harvard for his master's degree in literature. Tom Dabney said, "I took courses under, among others, George Lyman Kittredge. I felt that Harvard at that time had no one in literature superior to Sewanee's John Bell Henneman, either as scholar or as inspiring teacher."

Thomas Ewing Dabney '05 to ABC. *I can't recall the date.*

MEDICAL DEPARTMENT

A LVIN W. SKARDON '98 told his son that when he was at Sewanee the medical students would dress up their cadavers and seat them in life-like poses at the second-floor windows of Thompson Hall in order to frighten freshmen.

Dr. Alvin W. Skardon (his son) to ABC, June 14, 1963.

FIREWORKS

Breslin Tower was a good place to be from, or that is, Eph Kirby-Smith and I thought so a few seconds after the New Year of 1904 had been born. Eph had procured a stick of dynamite and suggested that we attach a fuse and cap with the idea of throwing it off the tower so as to give the few remaining people on the Mountain a thrill. We cut the fuse at what we thought was the right length so that the dynamite would explode in the air. However, our calculations must have been wrong for the explosion occurred on the cement walk below. It is amazing what a large hole can be made in cement with one stick of dynamite.

H. Harrison Sneed, Jr. '06 to W. G. deRosset '06, May 29, 1957.

LOVE IS NOT LOVE

Eph Kirby-Smith '07 had returned to Sewanee from Mexico and was preparing to return to Batopilas which was a seven-day burro ride from the railroad. He had recruited several Sewanee students to go with him including Louis Brooks '07, Merrick Sharpe '07 and others. While on the Mountain he had fallen madly in love with Polly Brooks who was engaged to George Watkins '06. As the wayfarers were boarding the train at Sewanee bound for Mexico, Polly broke into tears. She went back up the hill and told her sister, Catherine, "Phone Eph at the Franklin House in Cowan and tell him I'll marry him if he will come back." Ephraim mounted a horse and galloped back to Sewanee. After frantic preparations on the part of the whole community, the wedding was held the following day, and Polly left with Ephraim. They met the rest of the group in New Orleans and there continued to Mexico.

Eric P. Cheape '10 to ABC, March 27, 1963, checked with Mary Brooks Kirby-Smith. *After Eph's death, "Miss Polly" became a favorite matron in Hoffman and other halls, among her duties locating lodging for dates on dance weekends.*

THE BEST POLICY

JACK SHAFFER '07 with Lucien Memminger '00 and theolog Ed Johnston '08 went to Jeff Davis's Saloon in Winchester for a round of drinks. On the train coming back up the Mountain, they spotted seminary professor Haskell DuBose. There was a deal of confusion as the two undergraduates tried to hide the seminarian. DuBose was too alert for them and announced that Johnston would be punished by having to report the incident to his bishop. The elderly diocesan of Missouri, Daniel Sylvester Tuttle, was quite deaf. During holidays Johnston visited him and said, "Bishop, I've been drunk." The bishop queried, "Lost your trunk?" Johnston replied "Sir, I've been drunk." The bishop closed the matter with a wave of his hand. "Don't worry. I'll write the railroad and try to locate it." On his return Johnston said, "I told him twice, and that was enough."

J. Jackson Shaffer '07 to ABC, May 31, 1952.

BREAKING AND ENTERING

WHEN JACK SHAFFER was a student at Sewanee, he and Eph Kirby-Smith decided they owed it to themselves to dispose of one of the late General's kegs of blackberry wine which had been in the basement of Powhatan for about ten years. They came up with a magnificent strategem to outwit Miss Cassie [Mrs. Kirby-Smith]. Operating only at times when she was away from the house, they painstakingly chipped away the mortar from one of the sandstone blocks forming the foundation of the house. They were then able to enter from the outside, replace the stone, siphon all they could hold, crawl out, replace the stone, and stagger away. Shaffer declares that they kept up the routine until the contents of the keg had completely disappeared. A check with Dr. Rennie Kirby-Smith brought a guarded response. "It could have happened," he said.

J. J. Shaffer '07 to ABC, August 19, 1962.

RAGTIME

D R. JAMES T. MACKENZIE '11 of Birmingham was a bibliophile, with outstanding collections of hymnals, early operas, and Japanese paper, as well as being one of the most famous metallurgists in the world. As a student he was better known as an extremely versatile organist. In 1911 he played as an offertory in All Saints' Chapel "Alexander's Ragtime Band" with such skill that only a few amused choir members recognized it.

Gen. Godfrey Cheshire '14 to ABC, May 5, 1954.

ROLL CALL

A T SEWANEE in 1914 there were three students named Bowden. One of them, Carleton, who became a Rhodes scholar, was called Booden. A second one, Edwin, pronounced his name in the usual way, Boughden, and the third, Paul, pronounced his name in the Virginia manner, Boden. It happened that all three had one class together, History. The roll customarily was called Booden, Bowden, Boden.

Rev. Paul D. Bowden '16 to ABC, April 15, 1953. *A scholarship in his memory, established by his wife, aids ministerial students in college or seminary.*

BOTTLES

W HEN BISHOP KNIGHT's house burned the students knew that he had a good supply of wine in his cellar. The more energetic of them were able to salvage the entire contents of the wine cellar, though some of his fine books were lost in the flames. It is reported that not all of the wine found its way back to the Bishop after the fire.

Joe Scott '17 to ABC, June 10, 1954.

WHEN THE WATER'S RUNNING

W HEN FRANK A. JUHAN was proctor at "Old Hoffman" the building, whose insurance proceeds were used to build the present Hoffman Hall, was considered a very desirable dormitory. Today its attraction is hard to understand because the toilets were located in privies beyond the present Sigma Nu site. The single shower bath in the basement seemed to be the great attraction. In 1909 when the future bishop was making his rounds, he came across the distracted matron who reported that a student had just raided her ice box. Proctor Juhan set out to find the culprit. He made a complete search of the building with no results. He finally decided to go back into the basement just for a final check. He did so and heard the shower running. He pulled aside the curtain and found Eugene Field '12 of Calvert, Texas, in the shower with his clothes on and with the goodies in his arms. Field was let off with a reprimand after it was ruled that his offence was a prank rather than an honor council charge.

Bishop Frank A. Juhan '11 to ABC, February 5, 1961.

CONCENTRATION

I N 1907, Bishop Juhan, John Brown Cannon '94, and George B. Myers '07 went on a trip to the East. It was the first for all three of them. They took a Hudson River boat to West Point. It was full of Vassar College girls. Juhan and Cannon deployed themselves among the young ladies, but George Myers read philosophy. He became so engrossed in his book that when the boat docked at West Point, he failed to get off and was taken upstream to the next stop, Newburgh, whence he had to walk back to West Point to rejoin his companions.

Bishop Frank A. Juhan '11 to ABC, November 1, 1956. *All three are honored in Sewanee buildings—a gymnasium, a dormitory, and Bairn· wick, the former Myers home.*

TELEGRAM

SURELY ONE of the most perplexing telegrams of the decade of the 1930's arrived at Indianapolis from Sewanee. The text was as follows: YOUR SON JACK AND MY SON JOHN HAVE BURNED A HOUSE DOWN. DAMNDEST THING I EVER HEARD OF. It was signed R. M. Kirby-Smith and addressed to O. N. Torian, both MDs and contemporaries at Sewanee. The two culprits, neither with a pre- or post-history of arson, were John Kirby-Smith and John Potten Torian, known as Jack. Toward the cemetery there had stood for quite a spell a small, vacant, and probably worthless dwelling. The depression was in full swing, many huts and houses around Sewanee were tumbling into ruin, and it is at least possible that the two young gentlemen thought of themselves in heroic terms—ridding society of a local blight or creating jobs for the jobless. At any rate there was a blaze. All claimants were satisfied, no lives lost. Jack and John burned down no more houses, as far as is known.

ABC, conversations with both parents.

SPEED

AT THE famous Tuckaway Inn fire, student Jack H. Gibbons '24 arrived in tuxedo from what had apparently been a very convivial party. Dean George M. Baker, perceiving his condition, escorted him back to his room in Benedict Hall and put him to bed. Hurrying back to the fire, he found Gibbons there ahead of him, but in his street clothes.

Dr. George M. Baker to ABC, about 1960. *One has to be careful about place names at Sewanee. The "Benedict Hall" of this story was before and after known as "Fulford," the residence of Vice-Chancellors Quintard, Wiggins, Guerry, Green, McCrady, Bennett and Ayres, but for a time it was named for Dr. and Mrs. Cleveland K. Benedict of St. Luke's. They are honored in the newer stone Benedict Hall, a women's dormitory farther up University Avenue. Likewise, the first Sewanee Inn was a frame building on the site of its stone successor, now Elliott Hall, while Sewanee Inn is now the motel complex off the golf course.*

WOODEN PIGSKIN

Football BEGAN at Sewanee in 1891. A group of students had been on Hardee Field kicking a round ball, playing what they called football but what was really a form of soccer. They departed the field and took their ball with them, leaving eight or ten students without a ball. Ellwood Wilson '92 and Arthur M. Shepherd '94, both of whom had played football at eastern prep schools, offered to teach the others the new game. Among those taking part that first day were Frank E. Shoup '91, James B. Wilder '94, Charles M. Tobin '95, Ses Cleveland '92, R. M. Kirby-Smith '95, and Louis Tucker '92. They picked up a piece of wood, passing it from center to quarterback, as they practiced some simple plays. Next day the same group with a few others, and this time with a ball, scrimmaged at a field where Bairnwick now stands. After a couple of weeks a game was scheduled on November 7 with Vanderbilt. Sewanee lost. Then they played Tennessee in Chattanooga and won. The final game of the season was again with Vanderbilt and again Sewanee lost. The players bought their own uniforms, shirts laced up the front and very little padding in the pants. They put leather cleats on their regular shoes. There were no headgears or shoulder pads. Kirby-Smith hurt his back before the first game and was not listed among the players for that first season.

Dr. R. M. Kirby-Smith '95 to ABC, July 7, 1954.

RECORDS

Sewanee's four undefeated football teams were coached by J. G. Jayne in 1898, Herman Suter in 1899, and Shirley Majors in 1958 and 1963. Captains were Dana T. Smith for 1898, Henry G. Seibels for 1899, Andrew Finlay for 1958 and Robert Davis for 1963. In 1958 there were two alternate captains, Walter Wilder and James Gibson, and in 1963 there were three, M. L. Agnew, Larry Majors, and James Cofer.

ABC, The Archives.

THE IRON MEN OF SEWANEE

"*A*rthur," *Coach Walter Bryant grumbled one day, "why don't you ease up writing about those old Sewanee teams? Tell us about today's teams."*

In violation of Walt's admonition and thinking that there might be young people in kindergarten who haven't heard, I render herewith the Tale of the Team of Ninety Nine. Forgive me, Coach.

Sewanee's team of 1899, whose captain, the late Henry G. Seibels, is one of three Sewanee stars to make the National Football Hall of Fame, compiled a record which probably will never be equalled. It won 12 straight games and piled up 322 points to the opponents' 10 to become champions of the South. Five of the games were won in six days on a 3,000 mile road trip, perhaps the most gruelling road trip ever undertaken by an American team.

Backbone of the '99 team was a group of seven lettermen from the '98 squad which, also undefeated, had closed the season with a brilliant victory over Vanderbilt. Gloom came with the news that Captain-elect Dana T. Smith of Omaha had gotten married and would not return. The brand-new and untried coach, Herman Suter of Princeton, came on deck September 11 with a squad of 25 reporting.

Due to a disagreement over division of the prospective gate receipts, Vanderbilt did not meet Sewanee in '99. Luke Lea '00, Sewanee's manager, more than made up for this by arranging a schedule which showed more ambition than prudence. Lea, in 1910, was the last U. S. Senator from the state of Tennessee to be elected by the legislature. As a colonel in World War I, he led the madcap attempt to kidnap the Kaiser from his Dutch retreat after the hostilities.

Early season victories over Georgia (12-0), Georgia Tech (32-0), Tennessee (36-0), and Southwestern (54-0) established Sewanee as the team to beat in the South that year. Then on November 7 a 21-man travelling squad boarded a special sleeper to begin the incredible journey of triumph. Among the squad's most valued equipment were two barrels of Tremlett Spring water, calculated to offset dietary changes and inactivity during the long trip. The University of Texas went down (12-0) on the afternoon of November 9 in Austin. Sewanee prepped for that game with a light workout during a morning stop at a wayside station. After the game the visiting squad went to a dance, then boarded for Houston. There on November 10 Texas A & M tumbled 12-0, and on Saturday it was Tulane 23-0 in New Orleans.

Sunday the team went sightseeing, then sailing on Lake Ponchartrain, and to a play in the French Quarter before boarding the sleeper which hooked onto a Baton Rouge-bound train. There Sewanee plastered L.S.U. 34-0. The journey was beginning to tell by Tuesday when Sewanee only beat Ole Miss 12-0.

The squad rang up Sewanee's all-time record score by beating Cumberland 71-0 before playing the roughest game of the year when the Iron Men eked out a victory 11-10 over Auburn. To their respective dying days the Sewanee players vowed that the referees were tougher than the Plainsmen. With the SIAA crown safely stowed away, Coach Suter got in touch with his former roommate at Princeton, J. G. "Lady" Jayne, who had piloted North Carolina to an undefeated regular season (after having coached Sewanee's undefeated team of '98 and lined up Suter for his job when he left). The South's first post-season game was arranged for December 2 in Atlanta. The game was a see-saw with no touchdowns on either side. Ringland F. "Rex" Kilpatrick kicked an impossible goal for five points—the way a field goal was scored in those days. Incredibly enough, there is in the archives an action photo of that kick which won the championship of the South.

Ten of the twelve games were against conference teams, giving Sewanee the all-time record for (1) most conference games played and (2) most conference games won in a single season. Of the starting lineup, eight men were chosen on various All-Southern selections, also a record.

Sewanee Alumni News, February 15, 1949. Research by James Gregg, Jr., '48.

HALL OF FAME

Sewanee's three players in the National Football Hall of Fame are Henry G. Seibels '99. Henry D. Phillips '04, and Frank A. Juhan '11. Twenty-five players won All-Southern selections between 1899 and 1917.

ABC.

EVERYBODY BUT VANDY

T HE GREAT football teams of 1898 and 1899, both undefeated, had attracted so much comment from the sportswriters that Edmund C. Armes '13 determined to write about some other teams, less well known, which he felt were just as great. He chose the decade which ended his freshman year—1900 to 1909—and made these points.

This period (said Armes) produced the most scintillating individual stars of any ten-year period—Aubrey Lanier, Henry Phillips '04, Lex Stone '09, Chigger Browne '11, Scribo Scarbrough '07, Frank Juhan '11, and others. In this decade Sewanee won 61, lost 13, and tied 7. In seven of the ten years Sewanee lost only one game. In the two poorest seasons Sewanee won twice as many as it lost. During this period the enrollment averaged about 125 in the college, 20 in the theological school, and 150 in the then-flourishing medical school. During this decade there arose the saying "Vanderbilt beats everybody in the South and Sewanee beats everybody but Vandy."

In 1903 Sewanee went to Nashville for the last game of the season with a total of 174 points to her opponents' 0. Vanderbilt took the turkey 10-5. In 1904 Sewanee made the same trip with 179 to opponents' 10. Vandy won again 26-0. In 1905, a "bad" year, Sewanee had lost one and tied one before the final Thanksgiving tilt, and Vandy mopped up 68-4. Curiously enough, Sewanee supporters won more money that year because the victory-flushed Commodores' fans were betting Sewanee wouldn't score. The redoubtable John W. "Scribo" Scarbrough nearly caused a run on the Third National Bank with his 25-yard placekick for those lonely four points. In 1906 undefeated Sewanee went to Nashville with a whopping 211 points to 5. Again it was Vandy 20-0. In 1907 a team which many still consider Sewanee's greatest went to Nashville undefeated with 238 points to opponents' 10. By a ghastly fluke it was Vandy 17-12. In 1908 Sewanee made the annual trek with only one loss but with two ties and, of all things, squeezed out a tie, the third in a crazy season. Happy were the Mountain boys in 1909 when, with a win of 16-5 over Vanderbilt, the Purple was awarded the championship of the South.

Sewanee Football Stars since '99 by Edmund C. Armes '13, edited for posthumous publication by ABC, 1959.

93

GOLIATH AND THE CHIGGER

O N THE football teams of 1907-10 was a Goliath named Frank A. Faulkinberry '11, 240 pounds, 6'4" tall. Around his waist was strapped a leather belt with a handle rigged to it. Chigger Browne, 125 pounds, would hold on while "Big 'Un" charged through the scrimmage line. When giant and rider reached open field, Browne would dart away, frequently for a touchdown. Such helpful harness was soon outlawed.

ABC, edited from Edmund Armes' Sewanee Football Stars since '99. Faulkinberry's son became an equally great player for, sad to say, Vanderbilt.

BREW

T HE NIGHT before each game of the 1909 football season the members of the squad received one bottle of Guinness' stout. Heavy, sweet and dark, it was considered by Coach Harris Cope to be nutritious. After each game the players were allowed to drink two bottles of regular beer. The season was a success; Sewanee was declared "Champions of the South."

Bishop Frank A. Juhan '11 to ABC, August 12, 1957.

REWARD

B Y 1909 the Sewanee-Vanderbilt game had become one of the biggest sports attractions in the South. Clothiers of Nashville regularly offered prizes to players distinguishing themselves in the Thanksgiving game. In the famous contest of that year won by Sewanee, Red Moise dropped back to punt from the Sewanee 20. Frank Juhan, playing center, beat the ends to the receiver whom he tackled and who fumbled. Juhan scooped up the ball, started for the goal but was run down from behind by Brown of Vanderbilt on the two-yard line. The next play Chigger Browne called end-around, and Ed Finlay went over for the crucial score. Joe Morse had offered a hat to any player on either team who scored a TD, but he was so impressed by Juhan's play that he sent word by Aubrey Lanier that a hat would be held for Juhan too. For the rest of his life the bishop bought hats and suits from Morse, and the measurements never changed. Until the time of his death in 1967, the bishop weighed the same (165) as when in college.

Bishop Frank A. Juhan '11 to ABC, October 15, 1956.

THE SOUTHEASTERN CONFERENCE

Sewanee football teams have beaten Alabama 10 times, Tennessee 11 times, suffered far worse at the hands of Vanderbilt than any other rival, dealt more severely with Cumberland (15 wins, 1 defeat) than any other . . . done better than 50-50 with (among others) Ole Miss, L.S.U., Georgia, Georgia Tech, and Auburn . . . had a perfect record spoiled by Vandy 7 times, won 20 conference games in a row with a tie against North Carolina in 1900 breaking the string . . . and taken 44 consecutive conference beatings before retiring from the Southeastern circuit in 1939.

Sewanee Alumni News, February 15, 1949.

CASUALTY

WHEN AL COLE '38, later bishop of Upper South Carolina, was a student at Sewanee, he was very much interested in athletics, and he frequently would serve as chainman or timekeeper for varsity games. On one occasion Sewanee was playing an opponent on Hardee Field. The play was a long end run, and both teams swept down the sideline directly in front of the spectators. There was great excitement in the stands, the players on the bench were standing up near the sidelines exhorting their companions, and in due course the run was stopped several yards down the field. When everyone had been seated the only casualty of the play was observed. It was Al Cole, still clutching the pole, stretched out unconscious on the sideline.

Tom Claiborne '33 to ABC, March 25, 1955. *Hardee Field was named for Lt. Gen. William J. Hardee, who was present when Leonidas Polk was killed by enemy fire in 1864, and who visited Brig. Gen. Josiah*

Gorgas at Sewanee. In 1977 the field was renamed in memory of Ben Humphreys McGee '49, devoted alumnus and regent of the University.

FLIGHT

Malcolm Fooshee '18, Sewanee's fourth Rhodes Scholar, enrolled in the College in 1915. In defiance of nearly certain dismemberment, he went out for football and became, in due course, a substitute quarterback. In a breather game that year with Transylvania the Tigers got ahead, and Fooshee came in for his maiden appearance in a varsity game, weighing about 130 pounds soaking wet.

One must recall that in those days the whole game was played with one ball, and that ball had frequently been used before. It would get rounder and rounder as the seams stretched. On a fourth down, Fooshee was back in the safety spot when Transylvania punted. He was understandably excited. The kicker somehow punctured the ball, and in its course the pigskin took on the appearance of a child's balloon whose nozzle has been released. It zigged and it zagged as it arched toward the hapless Fooshee.

He was certain that it took a full two minutes to get back to him. Fullback Capers Satterlee '21, backing up the line, was watching Fooshee but couldn't see the ball. Capers remembers his own incredulity as Malcolm's head popped from side to side and he took a jump this way and the other. Fooshee meantime was having serious doubts about his own sanity.

He will never know how he caught the ball, but it was empty and limp. He looked at it in his hands. He was aroused by the sight of an end bearing down on him. Somehow, he still doesn't know why, he took the flabby object and slapped the opponent with it, dodging. The baffled end simply sat down on the field. Another end was now upon him, and Fooshee slapped him, darting for the shower room still clutching the deflated football. A third tackler brought him down near the sideline, and after some delay order was restored.

Rev. Capers Satterlee '21 to ABC, about 1962, confirmed by Malcolm Fooshee '18.

96

WILLIE SIX

Willie Sims' name was changed to Six early in his career. From a pile of football jerseys ready to be tossed out, he selected the least sleazy and appeared on the field with his water bucket and liniment wearing Number 6. "Six, come 'ere!" must have had echoes of Gunga Din—as a coach or player would call for this or that. The name stuck, and soon nobody called him Sims.

His memory was prodigious. He could recall for the rest of his life the shoe or helmet size of *every* player—not just the stars. Upon the humblest substitute's charley horse was lavished the same concern that Michael DeBakey would accord a heart-valve case.

Once a bald-headed alumnus from San Antonio appeared in front of the Supply Store. He hadn't been back for years. From a distance of fifty yards, Willie called out, "Hey, Mr. Red." Even Frank Gillespie '11 had forgotten that he once had red hair, but Willie had recognized him by his walk.

Another time after a rare game during the thirties when Sewanee had squeaked by an opponent, an aggressive alumnus of the other college directed some abusive remarks toward smallish Coach Gordon Clark '27. Willie Six came to Gordon's side, with his fists as big as hams, and said, "Mr. Clark, you jus' call him anything you want to."

The team went to play Army at West Point in 1934 and spent the night in New York City with sightseeing scheduled for the next day. Willie was told he could be on his own. He wandered around a bit and got lost. Train time approached, and no Willie Six. Search parties were dispatched, and soon one of them found Willie standing on a Manhattan corner. "Why," said one of the group, "didn't you look for the hotel? Weren't you scared?" "Naw," said Willie. "I knowed you'd find me."

James P. Kranz, Jr. '34 to ABC about 1968. Also many other notes.

The greatest Willie Six story had to do with a press interview at the time Willie retired and was honored on Hardee Field. Sewanee was playing a home game, post World War II, and a Nashville reporter pinned Willie down. This was not easy, because he normally never stopped as long as there was any work left to do.

97

"Willie," the reporter asked, "you've been trainer for hundreds of Sewanee teams in the last forty years. Which one was the best?"

Willie thought a moment and said, "The *best* team is the one a-comin' up."

Notes too numerous to chronicle but all verified by the late James Gregg, Jr. '48, Sewanee's greatest sports researcher, beside whom this author is an amateur.

TRAGEDY ON HARDEE FIELD

GEORGE RICE '29 of Houston was an exemplary young man in every way. A football tackling device fell on him causing concussion and spinal injury. He was rushed to the Vanderbilt Hospital where the doctor, after examination, told him he could not live. Two fellow students were in the room, much unnerved, and one of them offered him a cigarette. George said, "No, thanks, I'm in training."

David A. Shepherd '00 to ABC, November 26, 1954.

BY CYCLE FROM HOUSTON

TEN DAYS before the start of football practice at Sewanee in 1930, Julius French, varsity guard, left Houston on his fifteen dollar bicycle. He had known his parents would not approve. He asked them not to accompany him to the rail station, saying that parting always made him want to weep. He mailed his clothes, except for a small pack, put a can of oil and a wrench in his pocket, and was off. "I went alone, had a wonderful time, sleeping outdoors wherever darkness found me. I woke with the sun. One night it rained, and I slept on the porch of a grocery store. People were wonderful to me. The bike finally broke down in Cowan. I pushed it to the nearest farm house and gave it to a little boy, telling him how to fix it. I caught a bus up the Mountain, found myself one day early, and spent the night in a chair at the all-night filling station. The ride left me in good condition for football."

Julius G. French '32 to ABC, May 24, 1960.

WALLACE-ITES

T HE FOOTBALL team of Wallace University School came from Nashville in the fall of 1932 to play Sewanee Military Academy. The Wallace boys were accompanied by their faithful godfather, the distinguished Col. Overton Dickinson. There converged to witness the game a loyal assembly of fans from the surrounding coves, well supplied with the liquid product for which they were justifiably famous. The game was going badly for SMA, and Colonel Dickinson became a bit more exultant than the villagers thought appropriate to the occasion. As they moved menacingly toward the Colonel, there stepped forth his devout admirer, college sophomore Dudley Fort, a Wallace alumnus, who said, "These Nashville folks are friends of mine, and if you jump them, you got to whup me first." The onslaught was diverted and mayhem averted.

Dudley C. Fort '34 to ABC, some time ago. Dudley Fort was preceded at Sewanee by his father, Dr. Rufus Fort '93 and followed by his sons Dudley, Jr. '58 and Arthur '62.

BREAKFAST

W HEN COACH SHIRLEY MAJORS in 1958 presented Sewanee with its first undefeated team in fifty-nine years, jubilation ran riot. Dr. Gaston Bruton declared a holiday, but that was not enough. Students hatched a plot to serve all the players breakfast in bed. The plan worked perfectly except for one detail. Shirley was too early. He was up and gone when his butlers arrived. Bishop Juhan was not to be outdone. He made a breakfast appointment with Coach Majors at Thompson Union. Shirley guessed that he must be in for some gusta· tory delight. When he arrived, the Bishop handed him a sandwich, from which, on close examination, could be seen protruding a slip of paper. It turned out to be a check—and a generous one—inscribed in gratitude "to be used for something personal."

Elizabeth Majors to ABC, June 27, 1978.

DOGS

Florence Oates, in *It Should Happen to a Dog*, has covered the traditional Sewanee dog stories so well that they are not repeated here. Fitz Baker, buried in the Quadrangle, Hrothgar Myers, and other worthies are an integral part of Sewanee lore. Here are some dog stories less well known or unrecorded, placed with the students whose companions they were.

PIERCE GALLEHER

Bayard Snowden '03, for whom the forestry building is named, told about a wonder dog who had a sixth sense. Pierce, the pet of Mrs. Bishop Galleher, could predict precisely when the chapel bell was going to ring, and five or ten seconds before it sounded, he left home (where Johnson Hall now stands) and made a beeline for old St. Augustine's. If the door was about to be closed, he would almost go wild at the prospect of being late and would race up the aisle tripping students as he rushed to his place in the chancel.

J. Bayard Snowden '03 to ABC, September 10, 1956. *It was not until 1970 that I stumbled on a possible explanation. I returned to Sewanee from five years in New York and found office space in short supply. I was given a room in Breslin Tower right under the clock and immediately settled in. I began to notice the clearly audible sounds on the starting mechanism of the chimes and bethought myself of the story of Pierce. I think his ears were sufficiently sensitive to hear the grinding fifty or sixty yards away. Much as I regret to tarnish the ESP proclivities of one dog deceased, I will hold to my theory unless someone brings forth a better one.*

WITHOUT PRICE

Leonard Trawick, one of the most talented cartoonists in Sewanee history, drew for *The Purple* an immortal comic strip entitled "Sam's Brother" about a sagacious Sewanee dog who had no name of his own and no home except dormitory quarters. Sam's Brother had a girl friend, Pearl, who lived with the Robert S. Lancasters. Pearl understood English better than most seniors. During the summer of 1955, she heard the Lancasters plotting a trip abroad—his Fulbright lectureship in Iran. Incensed, and without so much as a by-your-leave, she packed up and moved to the home of Dr. and Mrs. Charles T. Harrison. Red and Tine both called on her, and on one occasion they took her back by car, but her mind was made up. She returned to her new quarters. Eleanor Harrison always maintained that Pearl, though deficient in morals, had great charm.

Mrs. Charles T. Harrison to ABC, October 28, 1955.

COVERED

F ATHER JOHN, a Sewanee notable whose name will be significant to some, belonged to Boo Cravens. The Volkswagen belonged to the late Dr. Joe Parsons, new-arrived surgeon from Alabama. For reasons which could only be explained by Father J or the VW, a tooting of horn by the latter provoked aggressive instincts in the former. Father John turned in the middle of the road, glared at the oncoming VW, and then rushed directly at it. Thanks to a slanting hood, the reverend canine was tossed gently in a twenty-foot loop to land on the pavement behind the car, without injury. The VW did not get off so lightly. Its fo'castle was dented and wouldn't open or close. Dr. Parsons inquired if there was insurance coverage. The agent responded, "Certainly. The dog bit the car, and it says right here that policyholders are protected in claims resulting from dogbite." Dr. Parsons was compensated by the insuror.

Marymor Sanborn Cravens to ABC, December 22, 1971, recalling an event of *circa* 1965.

SUICIDE SAVED

C OWYN, the Labrador retriever belonging to Colwell Whitney, was recovering nicely by Christmastime 1971. The handsome bitch fell or jumped from the ledge at room 308, Elliott Hall rear, at about 11 p.m. early in the month, and was missed an hour later. She was discovered moaning in the bushes behind the building and was immediately swathed in an electric blanket taken from the room she had been sharing with Whitney. Dr. Roger Way, University health officer, was routed from his bed to put a cast on the paw and to probe for possible internal injuries. Eowyn, named for a character in Tolkien, lived on to continue her intimacies with Calais Kirby-Smith Carruthers, Father John Morris, and others in the upper stratum of Sewanee canine society.

Colwell Whitney to ABC, Epiphanytide 1972.

RELIGIOUS TOLERATION

A LETTER FROM John B. Elliott to his brother Habersham dated August 11, 1870, reveals that even by then dogs were attending classes but were not allowed in Chapel. By 1962 the bars were completely down. At a laymen's conference a Sewanee dog came into the chancel to select his seat. A visiting layman stepped forward to remove him. Bishop William R. Moody of Lexington, the celebrant, turned from the altar to rule that the dog should remain. "Saint Francis would want it that way," he observed.

Fanny deRosset to ABC, August, 1962.

MUSIC STUDENT

THE PULITZER PRIZE-WINNING novelist James Agee lived on the periphery of the Sewanee campus for eight years. Father Flye first met him in 1919, Agee's second year at Saint Andrew's grammar school. The bright youngster was always ahead of his classmates, but few remember his devotion to music. He would ride his bicycle to Sewanee for piano lessons from Mrs. John Nottingham Ware, whose husband taught French in the college. Agee played classical music as long as he lived, and in his later years told Father Flye he wished he could have become a composer.

Father James Harold Flye to ABC, December 29, 1971.

HOMILETICS

Bᴵˢʜᴏᴘ Gɪʀᴀᴜʟᴛ Jᴏɴᴇs '28 tells a harrowing story of his first funeral service. In the seminary at Sewanee in 1928 he was assigned to the mission in Rowark's Cove. An infant, three weeks old, died in Akron, Ohio, and the body was sent back to Tennessee. Girault Jones went with the grandfather to Decherd where they met the train. In an old auto the future bishop carried the small casket on his lap to Rowark's Cove, arriving at 3:00 a.m. The grandfather, an imposing patriarch, drove up to a large house, knocked loudly on the door, and said, "Get up. This is a wake!" He similarly aroused neighbors in surrounding houses. About nine in the morning before the casket was taken to the church for a 10:00 o'clock service, the grandfather stood and said, "It's time to pass in review." Thereupon, the thirty or forty neighbors and friends stood up in the living room and marched twice around the casket, on the first round looking at the deceased infant and on the second round kissing it. This ceremony was repeated at the church, after which the grandfather turned to the depleted seminarian and said, "Now you can preach."

Bishop Girault M. Jones to ABC, July 8, 1956.

LOST OR STRAYED

A sᴇᴍɪɴᴀʀɪᴀɴ ɪɴ All Saints' Chapel in the 1920's was preparing to read the second lesson but did not know that it was a "turn around" lectern. He thumbed desperately through the Old Testament, could not find the next reading, looked up and said to the congregation, "Sorry, folks, it ain't here." The New Testament, of course, was on the other side of the gadget, facing the people.

Bishop Girault M. Jones '28 to ABC, July 8, 1956.

LATIN LOVER

W HEN THE not-yet-Reverend Fred Yerkes '35 came to Sewanee from St. John's College, he was well prepared in Latin and Greek. He had also some interesting little foibles. He would exasperate Professor Kirkland beyond all words by complacently knitting during a lecture, and then, when called on to read, would put down his needles and yarn, pick up his text, and read flawlessly.

Rev. Ben Meginniss '37 to ABC, about 1950.

CREDIT LINES

T OM MORRIS '45, erstwhile radio announcer, had entered seminary at St. Luke's and was conducting a practice service. As prefix for the Second Lesson, he intoned, "This passage is brought to you by II Corinthians." Afterward, Dean Fleming James asked, "Have you always been an Episcopalian, Mr. Morris?"

Bishop Girault M. Jones '28 to ABC, July 8, 1956.

GOBBLERS

A LFRED EDWIN MENNELL '27, Charles Wulf '26, and a couple of other students had slept in blanket rolls at the Cross and were walking back by SMA at dawn wrapped in their blankets. Mennell had a talent for imitating birds, and Col. DuVal Cravens had a yard full of turkeys. Alfred began gobbling. The turkeys came forth and trooped down the street. Mrs. Cravens opened the window and called, "Leave our turkeys be." The boys ran, and just before Mennell graduated he confessed to Mrs. Cravens that he was one of the culprits. She forgave.

Alfred E. Mennell '27 to ABC, April 13, 1973.

104

SAFE PASSAGE

John M. Ezzell was head proctor, living in Hoffman Hall with Sonny Poellnitz. Sheriff M. F. Jackson told him that some student had brought a ten-gallon keg of moonshine onto the campus for the forthcoming dance weekend. Sheriff Jackson suggested that if the head proctor, who had the right to enter rooms, would accompany him, they would find the keg. About 8 p.m. they set out. They started at Sewanee Inn [now Elliott Hall], went to Tuckaway, Cannon, Johnson, St. Luke's, and finally Hoffman. Sheriff Jackson said, "We don't need to search your room." But Ezzell insisted that his room should be searched just like the others. They opened both closet doors, saw nothing suspicious, and went on. Sheriff Jackson was mystified at the failure of the search. He was *sure* that his information was correct. The dance was a huge success, good spirits were obvious on all sides. It was only after Commencement that Ezzell learned the keg had been hidden the whole time in his own closet under his dirty clothes, stored there by his roommate and a couple of collaborators down the hall.

John M. Ezzell '31 to ABC, March 3, 1965.

AMEN

Until the cafeteria came, the ritual of blessing the food was inviolable at Sewanee, even though at times hunger overshadowed piety. At Magnolia Dining Hall in the 1930s, headwaiter Charles Douglass '34 found himself with a bishop on his hands and knew that His Grace should be exploited. Blowing the whistle, Douglass, in his still small voice and without the benefit of PA system, introduced the bishop and said same would give the blessing. Immediately following the two sentence introduction the entire student body chorused "Amen" and sat down. Whether or not the bishop actually said a blessing no one seems to remember.

ABC, from notes undated.

ARMY LIFE

N ED KIRBY-SMITH sat with his feet on the radiator in the spring of 1935, his junior year at Sewanee. His father, Dr. Rennie, had always said he hoped one of his four sons would go to West Point as their grandfather had done. Son Reynold had become an engineer. Henry had gotten his M.D., and John had announced his intention to go into physics. Came a telegram from a Senator asking the Doctor for the name of the son who wanted to go to the U. S. Military Academy. Ned said, "OK, send mine." Another telegram said, "Report to Fort McPherson for exams." Ned went and took the physical but declined to demean himself by taking the written exam. Instead he handed the officer his Sewanee transcript, fresh from the hand of registrar Tony Griswold, and said, "If this isn't good enough [he had just been elected to Phi Beta Kappa], I don't wanta go." Back in Sewanee a couple of weeks later he was astonished to receive another telegram saying he had been accepted at West Point. Thus began a military career which otherwise would probably have been that of a physician.

Col. Edmund Kirby-Smith '36 to ABC, August 5, 1972.

HELD UP BY CHINESE

F OR FOUR decades Fairmount College in Monteagle drew its clientele from all over the United States and from foreign countries as well. In 1909 a boy was born to the Burns family living near the school. When the news spread, young ladies vied to call and look. Among the first were two young Orientals, Mai Ling Soong and her sister Chung Ling. "May we hold the little American baby?" they asked. They could and did. That was several years before one became the wife of Chiang Kai-Shek and the other of Dr. Sun Yat-Sen.

Rev. Paul Dodd Burns '42 to Fanny deRosset, August 1, 1954.

The baby won his Phi Beta Kappa key at the University of the South and became head of Sewanee's first computer center.

HONORIS CAUSA

T HE FIRST honorary degree, Doctor of Civil Law, went in 1869 to the Rev. Francis W. Tremlett, rector of St. Peter's Church, Belsize Park, London, the University's commissary in England. The movement Tremlett inaugurated among English churchmen in 1867 resulted in sufficient funds to enable the opening of classes in 1868. Bishop Charles T. Quintard proposed Tremlett's degree at the first meeting of the board of trustees after the University opened. The degree chosen was, at Quintard's suggestion, that

> granted by the University of Oxford, the D.C.L. . . . This degree would be a distinguishing characteristic of the University of the South in America; all the other chartered Universities and Colleges in the United States alike conferring the LL.D. As ours is purely a Church University, it is proper that we should observe this distinction, and at the outset take our place in this particular, by the side of the Mother of the English schools of learning.

The second D.C.L. was given the Rev. Francis K. Leighton, Vice-Chancellor of Oxford University and canon of Westminster. The degree has been conferred on teachers, authors, bishops and other clergy, attorneys, businessmen, physicians, statesmen, editors, military officers, and college presidents. It was a favorite degree for the Commencement Orator and has been used as a special distinction for a clergyman who already had a D.D., when his attainments were not limited to his services to the Church.

The first doctorate in divinity was given in 1871 to the Rev. W.B.W. Howe, assistant bishop-elect of South Carolina, and the next to Bishop Robert W. B. Elliott of West Texas in 1874. A custom of awarding honorary degrees to all bishops on the board of trustees began in 1878. Major Fairbanks thought this "a rather wholesale way of conferring degrees."

The first doctorate in science went in 1904 to William Crawford Gorgas '75. The first LL.D. was awarded in 1880 to Edward Fontaine, a Confederate colonel, priest and Louisiana trustee. The doctor of letters (D.Litt.) was first awarded to a playwright, Edward Peple, in

1920. The B.Litt. was for many years an earned degree, though in 1915 George Fort Milton '91 received it *honoris causa.*

The first honorary Mus.D. was awarded to James Henry Lewis of Stames, England, in 1887. He was titled "registrar of music degrees for the University of the South in Great Britain," as part of Vice-Chancellor Telfair Hodgson's plan to create a music faculty to conduct examinations for bachelor's and doctor's degrees in music.

The Ph.D. has never been earned at Sewanee, but it was once planned to make it the equivalent of the masters of arts and sciences degrees combined. In 1887 the honorary Ph.D. was given to John B. Elliott, Sewanee teacher and physician, by then teaching at Tulane University, and in 1889 it was given to Caskie Harrison, former professor of classics who headed a boys' school in Brooklyn.

The doctoral hoods were first prescribed in 1872 and were in use by 1876, for Bishop Quintard recorded his pleasure at seeing one worn in Westminster Abbey by the officiating clergyman. The hoods have always been scarlet and "of the Oxford shape," though the Vice-Chancellor's crimson robe was the gift of friends at Cambridge University.

Elizabeth N. Chitty, drawing on the researches of Helen A. Petry and Rainsford Glass Dudney, *Sewanee Centennial Alumni Directory.*

RECITAL

T HE FOOTPEDALS of the organ in All Saints' Chapel could be manipulated from inside the works back in the 1940's. A freshman from Texas, plied with ghost stories, was sent to retrieve a book left on the organ bench by an upperclassman. By pre-arrangement, a conspirator was ready. The clouds were blowing through the rafters, there were no lights, and the nervous lad approached the vacant seat. The organ pealed forth, and the freshman fled. Watchers were delighted.

Mrs. Maryon Moise to ABC, May 20, 1957.

THE LONG WALK

A SUMMONS IN 1946 from Vice-Chancellor Alexander Guerry was a call from on high, no less—or at least so thought William E. Kelley '44. He had received the call in front of The Union from a sharply divided contingent of postwar students, mostly vets.

Former army pilot Kelley suspected that the gentleman he could see on the front porch of Fulford Hall had heard sounds of a low flying plane over the quadrangle an hour earlier and that this might be the subject of the forthcoming confrontation, but he hoped not.

Matter of fact there had been some betting going on for two or three days, and the stakes had become astronomical—a hundred dollars or more. On one side were those who believed that Lt. Bill Kelley could fly a plane between the Chapel and Science Hall (the space was open then), and there were those who bet it couldn't be done.

All of them knew in their hearts that Dr. Guerry's underground would know all, but somehow the VC had not heard the details before Kelley left the Mountain for the Cowan airfield to take off in a rented, fourth-hand Stearman two-seater bi-plane. Kelley was airborne before Guerry got the word.

Kelley approached his aerial project with caution. He circled to check out the height of the tree on the quadrangle which he would have to dive by and calculated the maneuver which might, just might, get him back up over the trees beyond. Unknown to Kelley, Guerry was observing the stunt from the fateful front porch. The errant pilot did what had to be done. He approached from the east, over Magnolia Hall, after having noted that the steam from the Sewanee Laundry was being blown from the west. He wanted to fly into the wind. He came through at the height of the roof of Science Hall, standing on his left wing tip, at 120 m.p.h., pulled up into a chandelle to the left, and off he went. The gambler spectators were ready to receive him with The Summons when he got back from Cowan.

Kelley took the Long Walk—from University Avenue to the Vice-Chancellor's home—dreading every step. There followed a conversation—highly privileged—which is revealed here for the first time.

Dr. Guerry was a master of suspense, and it was a couple of minutes before Kelley gleaned that he *might* not be shipped home. Dr. Guerry wanted to know exactly how the maneuver had been planned. He thought it a splendid exhibition. "Reminded me of Alex Junior," he murmured. (Alex had been a photo reconnaisance pilot in the Pacific, flying the suicidal P-38.) Guerry could not have been more eager to talk about the whole thing. The guys over at the Union were anguished over what was happening to Kelley. A prison sentence perhaps—certainly expulsion and disgrace.

As Kelley shook hands and left the porch, Dr. Guerry entered Kelley's hall of immortals by saying in effect, "It was a great stunt but don't tell the students across the street." Kelley kept the faith—until now.

William E. Kelley '44 to ABC. Long time ago, confirmed recently.

COAT AND TIE

It was a mid-afternoon in 1941. John Maury Allin had shouldered his trash bag and set out with pointed stick on his regular campus cleaning project. It was one of several ways in which the future Presiding Bishop earned money for his college expenses. On this day he decided he would go out the road to the Cross, spearing paper as he went and then tidy up the area around the monument at University View. He was ready to start back when he thought that he might as well burn his load of trash on the spot. He set a fire before noticing how very dry the grass was. In seconds the circle was enlarging dangerously and he had visions of being tried for arson. In his mind's eye he saw forest fires raging out of control. He started beating the fire with his trash bag but that was not enough. He took off his coat and with that gradually conquered the fire when it had reached a diameter of about twenty feet. As he walked back he reflected that he had identified a pragmatic justification for the tradition of wearing a coat at Sewanee but to this day can think of only esthetic justification for the tie. That, however, is enough, he thinks.

Bishop John M. Allin '43 to ABC, April, 1978.

IT TAKES TIME AT SEWANEE

THE FIRST references to the admission of women to the University came in 1896 when Bishop Gailor proposed to the trustees that a committee study the awarding of degrees to women. The following year a summer school of music was conducted for "both sexes," though the women were not matriculated and did not sign the ancient book which listed every student since Charles Massey Fairbanks in 1868. In 1899 Gailor asked again for study of female admission to graduate courses —medicine, law, pharmacy—but the committee on the Academic Department reported itself so divided on the subject that the matter was referred back to the board of trustees. Leading the opposition was the Rev. Hudson Stuck of Dallas, a lifelong bachelor, while the Vice-Chancellor, Benjamin Lawton Wiggins, said that he was in sympathy with admitting competently prepared women.

In 1912 a Woman's College was chartered, and in the Commencement procession of 1913 Miss Laura Drake Gill of Barnard College marched as the dean of the new college. She thought she had located a benefactor who would build and endow the college, but the plan collapsed. In 1920 the first women were matriculated in the summer session, and in 1946 wives of veterans were allowed to enroll. The first degree-seeking women matriculated in the college in the fall of 1969, and the first earned degrees were awarded in 1971 to women who had transferred from other colleges and been in residence two years.

Sewanee coeds were admitted fifteen months after the decision was made by the trustees, leaving a distracted administration to worry about details such as laundries, kitchens and shower curtains. Kenyon College, which opened to women at the same time, had spent thousands of man-hours in conversations with consultants and fund-raisers. One approach seemed to work as well as the other. At both campuses women came, stayed, and were happy. As were the men.

ABC, references to *Proceedings of the Board of Trustees* as indicated.

FIRST COED

Miss Eleanor Walter Thomas, sister of Bishop Albert S. Thomas '98, wrote her nephew:

"'I have the distinction of being the first woman student at the University of the South, not officially registered in the summer of 1901 but receiving grades in six English courses. I never had more thorough teaching than from Professor John Bell Henneman."

Miss Thomas went on to receive her Ph.D. and became head of the English department at Western Reserve in Cleveland, which awarded her a D.Litt. on her retirement.

Eleanor W. Thomas to Hasell LaBorde, November 12, 1954.

ON TARGET

During my days on the Sewanee Club circuit, I liked to tell several stories which illustrated the high productivity of outstanding leaders by the University of the South. One of my favorites was this. On my first visit to Atlanta as Alumni Secretary, I found in the receiving line the bishop of the diocese (John Moore Walker '14), the recent governor (Ellis Arnall '28), and the commanding general of the Third Army (Alvan C. Gillem '12), rather good representation from so small a college in another state.

Then in 1950 I went to New York to find that the presiding officer of the meeting was J. Albert Woods, '18, then of W. R. Grace and Co. and later president of Commercial Solvents and Courtaulds, North America. Reading the club's necrology was Niles Trammell '17, president of NBC, and being memorialized were the bishop of New York (William T. Manning '91), the Army's top authority on military law (Gen. Edmund R. Beckwith '10), and a dean of Columbia University's School of International Law (Huger W. Jervey '00).

Back at Sewanee we were preparing the *Centennial Alumni Directory*, and I found that Sewanee alumni were thinly scattered in the Northwest, perhaps thirty in three states. However, they included the bishop of Idaho (Frank A. Rhea '13), the governor of Nevada (Vail Pittman '99), and the U. S. senator from Washington (Harry P. Cain '29).

ABC, speech notes.

112

CHAPTER FIVE

BISHOPS

BEGGAR ABROAD

DURING HIS tour of Great Britain, in the course of one hundred and twenty days, he [Quintard] preached one hundred fifty-five sermons and made numerous short addresses. He made such a tour in our parent island as perhaps no other American ever did.

Clipping from the Nashville *American,* October 1876, in Charles Todd Quintard Diary, volume 8, day of month not discernible. *This was the Bishop's second trip. On the first (1867) he preached two hundred fifty times in one hundred eighty days. He often said that the appropriate inscription for his tombstone was from Luke 16:22: "And it came to pass that the beggar died."*

BETTER THAN LAST YEAR

COMMENCEMENT DAY—Ye great day. Everything was admirably arranged and ye most exact order was observed. Bp. Gregg wore ye Doctor's Hood for ye first time. Ye Venerable Chancellor [Green] is far too infirm to preside at such an occasion. He made ye graduates of schools B.A.'s & M.A.'s without at all knowing what he was at. I asked him before ye service to allow ye V.C. Hodgson to recite ye formula and he confer diplomas and degrees; but he insisted on it that he knew his lines better than last year & he must do ye whole duty.

Charles Todd Quintard Diary, August 2, 1883.

ABSENT

Dear Brethren:

Only a supreme sense of duty detains me from you at this time. . . .
I came to this land to accomplish a great work for the Church, not
only in the Diocese of Tennessee, but in all our southern dioceses.
Nay, may we not hope that the University of the South will be a blessing to our whole country, north as well as south. My work here is not
yet done. I must remain longer. . . . It is the first time that I have
ever been absent from a convention . . . since I took my seat as a lay
delegate in dear Bishop Otey's time.

Bishop Charles Todd Quintard in a letter from England to the Clergy
and Laity of the Diocese of Tennessee, in convention assembled, May
7, 1876. *The University of the South ought never to expect a bishop
to place it before his own diocese . . . but it is interesting to know that
at least one bishop on one occasion did.*

EXTRAVAGANCE

M RS. GEORGE QUINTARD, sister-in-law of the Bishop and daughter
of Morgan of the large shipping interests, said, "It is fine to have a
bishop in the family, but it is an expensive luxury."

Queenie Woods Washington to ABC, January 20, 1952. *When Morgan
died, Bishop Quintard lamented in his diary what a pity it was that he
didn't leave some of his $20 million to Sewanee.*

LIES

B ISHOP QUINTARD was telling a group of people about Sewanee's
early days, and erred on a date. A listener upbraided him for being
wrong—a bishop should be right about *everything*. Quintard humbly
confessed his error but complained, "If I can't tell a small lie once in
a while, what's the use of being a bishop!"

David A. Shepherd '00 to ABC, December 17, 1954.

PRESIDENT HAYES

THE GOVERNOR (of Tennessee) invited me to meet the President at his room in the Capitol. . . . The Governor entered the room with the president on his arm and introduced me. For a few moments we had the room to ourselves. . . . Then came the Secretary of State, Mr. Evarts, with Mrs. Hayes, the Postmaster Genl. Mr. Key, and Governor Wade Hampton of South Carolina. Governor Hampton gave me his arm and the party went to the East front of the Capitol. . . . Mrs. Hayes very graciously seated me by her side, on a sofa reserved for the ladies. . . . (Hampton) was enthusiastically cheered, as was the Presdt.

Charles Todd Quintard Diary, September 19, 1877.

Accompanying clipping said "30 or 40 thousand people were present." It is curious that Quintard does not mention that Hayes was an alumnus of an Episcopal College—Kenyon in Ohio.

VICTORIAN STOLE

ON THE lawn at Tuckaway during one of the several summers he spent at Sewanee before his death, the Rev. Walter A. Dakin told how Bishop Quintard gave him a stole at his ordination. Said Quintard, "This was given me by Queen Victoria, and if you wear it you will surely become a bishop." Father Dakin, then about 90, quipped, "I'm still waiting."

Rev. W. A. Dakin '98 to ABC, July 29, 1953. *The gentle priest didn't attain the ecclesiastical immortality of the episcopacy, but he did have a room at St. Luke's named in his memory—given by his grandson Tennessee Williams.*

UNREPENTANT

BISHOP QUINTARD went back to Connecticut after the war and suffered the indignity of not being invited to preach in his own family's church in Stamford. To ease the offense, someone secured an invitation for him to preach in another church in the same city. He did. As he was waxing eloquent he noticed one old lady dissolved in tears. Afterward, he asked if his sermon had come especially close to her and she said, "No, it wasn't the sermon. I just couldn't bear the sight of the son of my old friends come back to his home town wearing a rebel flag around his shoulder." Bishop Quintard was wearing his Cambridge hood.

Rev. Henry Bell Hodgkins '26 to ABC, July 31, 1952.

THEN CAME SHERMAN

"PETERS," SAID Confederate Chaplain Charles T. Quintard one morning in 1864 after a discussion concerning the need for an Episcopal Church on the north side of Atlanta, "If you furnish the money I will detail a squad of soldiers to build the church, and we will hold services."

Ralph Peters agreed to this proposition, and St. Luke's Church was established on Walton Street. The future Bishop Quintard appointed himself rector, and the congregation had worshipped there just seven weeks when the building was burned by Sherman's Army.

Atlanta Constitution, February 16, 1898. The Ralph P. Black, '01 golf shop at Sewanee is named for Ralph Peters' grandson, who played on the football team (12-0-0) *of 1899.*

EPISCOPAL PROFANITY

GENERAL B. FRANK CHEATHAM, whose daughter Medora lived in the house next to Thompson Union, did not hesitate to use profanity in the height of battle, but Bishop-General Polk would not. On one occasion General Polk exhorted his men: "Now, boys, give them what Cheatham would say."

Queenie Woods Washington to ABC, November 14, 1951.

CLERGY BEWARE

I N THE Torian Archives can be seen a handsome 16th century ceremonial halberd discovered by the author when he bought the Mac-
Kellar house from the University in 1948. The stone-and-shingle Fulford Cottage was built by Bishop Quintard's son George. The Quintard diary reveals that the halberd was given him by the Rev. Canon
Moore of Lincolnshire. The Bishop wrote that he could think of no
other use for it than as "a pastoral staff for disciplining ecclesiastical
Ku Klux" in Tennessee.

Quintard Diary, July, 1885.

PROFILE

B ISHOP WILLIAM MERCER GREEN—for he has never acquiesced in the
the addition by his sons of the letter E to the name—was born in 1796.
He is [1885] the oldest living Bishop in this country, if not in England, and is second to but one in seniority of office—the Rt. Rev.
Bishop Lee of Delaware—though the latter is his junior by nine years
in point of age. Bishop Green was a contemporary of George Washington, so to speak, for nineteen months, a fact which conveys to this
generation almost a supernatural longevity. . . . He was made Bishop
of Mississippi in 1850, and is still in active service, being in fact at
this moment on the way to Mississippi from his mountain home at
Sewanee upon an official visitation. The venerable Bishop was Professor of Belles-Lettres at Chapel Hill from 1837 to 1849, being in the
latter year elected to his present high position. During the occupation
of Jackson by the Federal army, his home was razed, his library and
all his possessions were swept away. He removed to Columbus and in
1866 fixed his home at the little mountain village of Sewanee, and
there he hopes to bring his labors to a close. He is the fourth Chancellor of the University, having been preceded by Bishops Otey, Polk,
and Elliott.

Clipping from the *Nashville American*, 1885. *Had Green lived a few
months longer, he would have become, by seniority, Presiding Bishop.*

WILLIAM MERCER GREEN: A LENTEN STORY

WHEN JENNY LIND, in the days of her triumph, was making a tour through America, she stopped at Natchez, at a time when the late Bishop Green was there. It being Lent, he felt it his duty to decline the invitation to attend her concert.

The next day his carriage met hers as she was being driven to the boat. He, wishing to assure her that the refusal meant no discourtesy but was simply a matter of conscience connected with the holy season, requested the driver to stop. The Queen of Song was so much impressed, that, alighting from the carriage and kneeling upon the bare earth, she begged his paternal benediction. A gentleman who was with the Bishop relates the incident as one of the most affecting he ever witnessed. The minister of God, standing bareheaded, laid his hand upon the head of the kneeling woman and prayed God's blessing upon her, that her wonderful art might redound to His glory, and that the voice so tuneful upon earth might one day sing the angels' song in Paradise.

From clippings in Sewanee Archives, undated, unidentified, about 1887. *The outstanding living authority on Jenny Lind, as well as on shaving mugs, antique ice skates, and cigar-store Indians, is W. Porter Ware '26 of Sewanee.*

MARRIFIED

ONE DAY I heard Bishop Green say "I marrified her." I did not ask then why he used that expression but was told later. A friend who had been in Europe congratulated him (the Bishop) on his marriage to a young woman about the age of his grandchildren. The Bishop was embarrassed and denied it. The man said, "But my brother said you told him you had married her." The Bishop replied "Henceforth I will *marrify* all who come to me to be joined in wedlock."

Queenie Woods Washington to ABC, November 14, 1951.

SLANDER

Dear Editor,

There have appeared lately some extracts from a forthcoming history of our late war, all of which I read with pleasure, except *one sentence*. Speaking of Mr. Jefferson Davis, you state that, at the time of his capture, he was attempting to make his escape in female apparel.

This slanderous story was gotten up at a time of high political excitement, when groundless rumors and disparaging statements were too readily credited by both sides. From time to time, the thing has been repeated by the vulgar and the ignorant. The friends of Mr. Davis have been willing to let it pass as undeserving of their attention. But when it appears that [you are] about to record your belief in that false and foolish story. . . . [Green goes on to say, in effect, "forget it."]

Bishop William Mercer Green to "Editor," June 15, 1885, from Sewanee. The clipping is torn but is obviously from Bishop Green, probably in Nashville *American*.

SALVAGED

T HE REV. WILLIAM WILBERFORCE LORD, pre-War trustee of the University of the South, was a man given to setting things right. Exploring a cemetery one day he read on a lady's tombstone the surprising inscription:

SHE HAD HER FAULTS

Poking around, he noted that an overgrowth of grass had covered the next line:

BUT WAS KIND TO THE POOR.

He had the stone raised at his own expense and set on a new base in order that the virtue of the deceased could be displayed.

Margaret Lord (Mrs. J. B.) Miller to ABC, December 9, 1953. *She was the last surviving daughter of a founding trustee.*

SAVE THE SMOKES

Bishop Richard Hooker Wilmer of Alabama was a heavy cigar smoker. When a new minister came into his diocese, he would always ask if he smoked. If the minister said no, Bishop Wilmer would congratulate him and would say, "I advise you to continue to refrain from this habit. I would not want you, however, to be overly pious in the matter and when you are offered a cigar, I suggest that you *not* refuse it. Instead, accept and save it for your Bishop."

Richard W. Hogue '97 to ABC, May 13, 1953.

REBUTTAL

Richard Hooker Wilmer of Alabama, the last member of the House of Bishops to espouse slavery as morally right, went back to Yale for a reunion with classmates. He was taunted for his rebel posture and decided to retaliate. He asked what book had done most to inflame the North against the South, and they agreed on *Uncle Tom's Cabin.* He pushed on: "Who is the finest character in the book?" Answer, "Little Eva." The bishop said, "She was a Southern lady." He continued: "Who was the most loyal character?" They replied, "Uncle Tom." Bishop Wilmer pointed out, "He was a Southern Negro." Then warming to his punch line, he queried, "And who was the worst person in the book? It was Simon Legree, of course—a Yankee." Presumably that stopped them in their tracks.

The same bishop, prior to his elevation to the episcopacy, served a small rural parish in Virginia. From time long past it had been fashionable for children to be baptized at home, on the plantation, privately. The Rev. Mr. Wilmer thought baptism ought to be in church. There was dissension which did not decrease when he announced from the pulpit a new and more liberal policy. Henceforth instead of declining all baptisms outside of church except *in extremis,* he would consider private baptisms in homes when there was a question of legitimacy.

David A. Shepherd '00 to ABC, April 15, 1955.

SOCIETY HILL

The tiny town of Society Hill, South Carolina, has been the birth-place of a Chancellor and two Vice-Chancellors of the University of the South. They were the Rt. Rev. Alexander Gregg, Bishop of Texas and Chancellor of the University (1887-1893), Benjamin Lawton Wiggins '80, Vice-Chancellor (1893-1909), and Benjamin Ficklin Finney '89, Vice-Chancellor (1922-1938).

The Rev. Alexander Gregg was rector of St. David's, Cheraw, when elected bishop. There he found the usual suspicion of Episcopalian pecularities flourished in his own home. His father finally said he would attend services at his son's church if he would not wear "those night clothes."

Alexander's father-in-law, Dr. Kolloch, did attend but regularly went to sleep during the sermon. When chided about it, he said that it was a compliment to Gregg: "I feel safe when you preach."

Gregg boosted attendance by keeping in his diary a record of parishioners who did not come to church. He would rush to call and would ask if they had been ill on Sunday.

Arthur Howard Noll, *Bishop Gregg of Texas* (Sewanee: University Press, 1912).

Among Gregg's unusual experiences as Bishop, few are as dramatic as his confirmation of a man and woman standing before the corpse of their daughter. She had asked them to join the church in her pres--ence, and they had delayed.

Alexander Gregg Diary, December 9, 1888, Texas Diocesan *Journal.*

ROBIN HOOD

Bishop Gregg covered the whole state of Texas, mostly by stage-coach, until the diocese was divided three ways in 1874. On one occasion, it is said that the stage was held up. In handing his watch to the highwayman, the Bishop said, "This watch has great sentimental value to me. Might I keep it?" The robber inquired, "Who are you?" Gregg said, "I am the Episcopal Bishop of Texas." The man put his pistol in his holster, handed back the watch, redistributed other loot to passengers, and told the driver to move on, saying, "I am an Episcopalian too."

Rev. Moultrie McIntosh '47, a collateral descendent of Bishop Gregg, to ABC, January 18, 1962. *Moultrie, this story is too good to be true, but I print it on your personal responsibility.*

BY RAIL

Bᴵꜱʜᴏᴘ Gᴇᴏʀɢᴇ Hᴇʀʙᴇʀᴛ Kɪɴꜱᴏʟᴠɪɴɢ was a very big man, weighing over 250 pounds, nearly six-and-a-half feet tall, and wearing enormous shoes. Once he boarded the train on a routine visitation and inadvertently got in a vacant berth assigned to someone else. The rightful owner demanded that the interloper be evicted, the porter protesting that there were other berths and that the traveller had gone to sleep. The man said, "If you don't disturb him, I will." Looking down he saw for the first time one of the bishop's size 18 shoes. Turning to the porter he said, "Where is that other berth?"

The bishop was not only big but absent-minded. He got on another train, and when his friend the conductor came, he couldn't find his ticket. The conductor said, "That's all right, Bishop. You can send it to me later. Where are you going?" The bishop said, "I don't know. It's on the ticket."

W. Clendenin Robertson to ABC, December 5, 1959.

SHERMAN'S CHOICE

A ᴅᴀʀɪɴɢ ᴄᴜʀᴀᴛᴇ was baiting the formidable Bishop Kinsolving in Texas and had the temerity to remind him of an observation credited to William Tecumseh Sherman. The doughty general said if he had

122

to choose between hell and Texas he would move to hell and farm Texas. Bishop Kinsolving replied, "Sherman got his choice. I'll take Texas."

Dr. Robert W. Daniel '35 to ABC, August 12, 1972.

UNCROWNED KING

A LOYAL LADY parishioner in a small Texas town was expecting Bishop Kinsolving but had to dash out for some last minute arrangements. She carefully instructed the maid to welcome the bishop if he came while she was away. On returning, she asked if the bishop had arrived. "Naw'm," said the maid. "Nobody came but a big crazy man who said he was Kin' Solomon. I slammed the door in his face."

Dr. Robert W. Daniel '35 to ABC, August 12, 1972.

DOPE

A T A trustees' meeting about 1902, Chaplain William Alexander Guerry proposed a resolution, supported by suitable oratory, that the sale of "dope'" (Coca-Cola) be prohibited. Students, pre-warned of this maneuver, delegated resourceful young Biddy Smith '03 to spy on the meeting. Under a window he heard various opinions concluding with a statement from Bishop Ellison Capers of South Carolina. He himself had imbibed three successive cokes, he confessed, and finding them of no effect whatever had returned to mint juleps. The motion was tabled.

Sterling S. Lanier to ABC, April 16, 1953.

BACK TO THE RAMPARTS

CHAPLAIN GUERRY, however, was not easily defeated. Came 1906 and with pro-Coke ranks thinned by absences, there arose Zadok Daniel Harrison to move that a special committee be appointed "to investigate the question of the sale of Coca-Cola . . . and of [its] harmfulness. . . ." This passed.

To guard against possible calamity between the annual sessions, the Bishop of Georgia moved further that since "from reliable statements . . . Coca-Cola is seriously detrimental to students . . . the Board urges that residents and students, and especially officers of the University, discourage the use of this beverage. . . ."

In 1907 the committee asked for another year in which to complete its research. In 1908 the report came in. "Evidence shows that a glass or bottle of Coca-Cola contains about the same quantity of caffeine as a cup of coffee or tea [and hence] that the Hebdomadal Board be directed to adopt such measures . . . as will most effectively prevent intemperate drinking of Coca-Cola and other like beverages." After discussion, which required extension of the hour of adjournment, the motion was passed.

In 1907 Chaplain Guerry was elected Bishop of South Carolina. With the departure of Coke's arch-enemy, strictures relaxed, and before long students were quaffing their dopes openly.

Trustees' Proceedings, 1906, 1907, 1908. Contributions from "Coke money" to Sewanee are numerous; to wit, Johnson Hall, Hunter Hall, the Wilkins Scholar endowment, and most of Guerry Hall—the last a delightful irony in view of the Bishop's ill-fated campaign.

LUCRE

T HE REV. FRANK A. JUHAN had just started preaching in his first little church in West Texas. The mission treasurer forgot to give him his stipend at the end of the month, and the future bishop was broke. On the first Sunday after he should have been paid, Juhan asked the treasurer before the service, "Can you lend me five dollars?" The treasurer loaned him five dollars. After the service Juhan returned it, and the treasurer expressed bewilderment. Juhan replied, "I always speak better when I have money in my pocket."

Bishop Frank A. Juhan '11 to ABC, June 15, 1960.

THE BISHOP ATE CROW

T HE REV. TELFAIR HODGSON was not a man of great ferocity, and his son Telfair was even less so. Strange then that it was left to a mild man to hang history's greatest public rebuke on Bishop Gailor. But it did happen, and in this wise.

There had been neighborly troubles across the fence, and Telfair was furious with Bishop Gailor. But since a fury with Telfair usually equalled in volume of terror a clearing of the throat by the Bishop, no one was uneasy when the Gailors came to chicken dinner on a bright Sunday. Several friends were in for the occasion, and, though the ladies had all been served, there was still plenty of the Bishop's favorite white meat on the Hodgsons' generous board. With pallid cheek but with firm hand, Telfair amputated the left drumstick of the starboard fowl, placed it on the Bishop's plate without a word and passed down the long table the one piece of chicken *everyone* knew the Bishop disliked. Miss Medora gasped, the guests recoiled, the Bishop looked unbelievingly, and for a brief moment, there was some likelihood that the diners would, as one man, bolt for cover. But no word was spoken, the Bishop made no motion, someone said something inconsequential, the equilibrium of the party was restored, and the Bishop silently ate every bite. It was a moment of great triumph for Mr. Hodgson. Old scores were settled.

David A. Shepherd '00 to ABC, November 18, 1951.

LOW EBB

E ACH SPRING in Memphis the Gailor family would get increasingly anxious to move to Sewanee for the summer. One day at lunch with only the Bishop, Mrs. Gailor, and daughter Charlotte present, the blessing was said, and not another word was spoken. It was hot, and spirits were low. Finally the dishes were cleared and out was brought dessert, the bishop's favorite, open-faced cherry tarts. Still glum, but brightening a bit, the bishop leaned over for a better look at the delicacy, and his glasses fell off his nose into the tart. He thereupon spoke the first word to be uttered since the invocation—"Damn!"

Dr. Robert W. Daniel '35 to ABC, October 1, 1953.

TENTATIVITY BANISHED

Bishop Thomas Frank Gailor was a man with a booming voice and very positive ideas. On matters about which most people would have only vague reactions, his mind was made up. On one occasion a friend asked him, "Bishop, how many is 'several'?" Without hesitation he replied, "Eight."

He was a ferocious competitor at bridge and loved to play the game. One of his regular partners was the late Mrs. Roy Benton Davis, whose stepson, though only twelve when she died of leukemia, remembers that the Bishop never played bridge on Sunday—until after 3 P.M.

Rev. Roy Benton Davis, Jr. '41 to ABC, July 9, 1972. *I only played bridge with the Bishop once. It was the summer of 1933. Partners were Charlotte Gailor and Robert Daniel. It marked me. I gave up bridge for life.*

EVEN WORSE

Mrs. Telfair Hodgson, Sr., asked Bishop Gailor, "Why do you always read your sermons?" Bishop Gailor explained that he rarely tried to speak extemporaneously, because he feared he might forget some of his principal points. The next Sunday, however, he preached without notes. Mrs. Hodgson apparently did not like his sermon. Afterward she commented unfavorably on it and said, "Were you using notes this time?" The bishop said, "No," and she said, "I was afraid of that."

Dr. G. M. Baker to ABC, July 4, 1956. *Gailor, like Winston Churchill, finally moved to the apex of his career as a great speaker by writing, memorizing, and then delivering without notes his addresses and sermons.*

126

SUSPICIOUS CHARACTERS

On July 29, 1913, at the Union Station in Cincinnati, Bishop Thomas Frank Gailor, his daughter Ellen Douglas, and her friend Stephanie English were detained by a corps of detectives on the suspicion that he was a swindler. The Bishop had been in New York for three weeks filling the pulpit of St. Bartholomew's Church on Madison Avenue. An amateur Sherlock Holmes aboard the parlor car of the Pennsylvania Railroad had been reading of a bogus Catholic priest who had been fleecing New York's innocent citizens and who on his "jobs" was invariably accompanied by two young women. The young man wired ahead to Cincinnati to have a delegation of the constabulary waiting for the suspect. The Bishop said, "I had alighted from the train to send a telegram when a young man first came up to me and then others and then began to ask questions. I told him I was a clergyman and presented my credentials, but there was considerable hesitation. Finally, Mr. George W. Brandt of the Havana *Post*, Dr. Lucas of Nashville and several Louisville gentlemen vouched for me, and the detective chief and others apologized." The Bishop added, "My daughter and Miss English thought it was a great joke."

New York *World*, July 30, 1913. Editor's Note. *The* World *should have known better. St. Bart's is on* Park *Avenue.*

CHAPLAINS

At a meeting of trustees about 1912 Bishop William Alexander Guerry was nominating a clergyman for the chaplaincy. He made a thirty-minute speech extolling the virtues of his candidate. Bishop Henry Judah Mikell of Atlanta arose and said to Gailor, who was presiding, "Mr. Chancellor, the gentleman of whom the Bishop of South Carolina has just spoken is in my judgment dull, heavy, stupid, and elephantine." Bishop Gailor boomed, "Why not add rhinocerosic?" The nominee was not elected.

Edmund C. Armes '13 to ABC, July 20, 1952.

TALL TALE TELLER

Dear Arthur:

You inquired about Pike Hall's story concerning Vice-Chancellor Knight and General Gorgas. Among Bishop Knight's tallest stories was how he, while Bishop of Cuba (with jurisdiction over Panama) had instructed General Gorgas on the problems at the Canal and how it was only through following these instructions that General Gorgas had succeeded where the French failed. The students took the story with more than the proverbial grains of salt.

Before and after the United States entered World War I, various universities raised ambulance units from their student bodies. The Sewanee unit was sent to Allentown, Pennsylvania, for training, but there it was forgotten. No officers were assigned; no uniforms issued. The men were simply assigned to tents and left in civilian clothes on their own. As time went on they saw other units properly organized, equipped, trained and sent away. Annoyance increased. Finally someone suggested that if Bishop Knight was such a close buddy of General Gorgas, why not write the Bishop to call upon the General to do something about it. Such a letter was prepared, signed by the men, and mailed.

Several days later carloads of high brass appeared. Uniforms were issued, not by supply sergeants but by captains and majors. A company was formed, and the men instructed in basic drill and parade commands. Within hours they were marched to the camp rail siding where they were stood at attention while a special car was pulled onto the siding and out stepped Bishop Knight, followed by General Gorgas. The Bishop quickly assumed military command, called for "Right hand salute" followed by "Stand at ease" and then told the men how he had received their letter with dismay and had immediately called upon his friend General Gorgas who had responded with dispatch. Knight assured the men that their patriotism would not be ignored and they would be among the first to sail for Europe.

To the men's incredulity General Gorgas then recounted his long friendship with Bishop Knight at Panama. He stated his success was due largely to the knowledge, insight, and advice of the Bishop. The men were completely floored. True to the Bishop's words the men set sail almost immediately, unfortunately with inadequate training and

128

inexperienced officers. Their service in France was arduous in the extreme. Many times in France the men kicked themselves for calling on the Bishop but they could not blame him. He exceeded all expectations.

Milton C. Trichel, Jr. '31 to ABC, March 11, 1957. Excerpts from letter.

CONVICTION

Some years ago at an annual Council of the Diocese of Florida, the Reverend Thomas Byrne (St. Andrew's, Panama City) offered the following resolution:

"Mr. Chairman, I move that a committee of three be appointed to determine the difference between the University of the South in Sewanee, Tennessee, and the Kingdom of God." The motion was seconded, but the Chairman—Bishop Juhan—did not call for a vote or appoint the committee. He thought there wasn't any difference.

Rev. Henry Bell Hodgkins '26 to ABC, June 25, 1958. *When the Bishop's Common was named, no surname was needed to identify whose dream it was. Likewise, the Domain is beautified by the Bishop's Crew, which he personally directed in his lifetime.*

SPINAL FUSION

Bishop Duncan M. Gray the First, of Mississippi '25, had an extremely sharp sense of humor. The Rev. Vincent Franks, rector of St. Andrew's, Jackson (later the Cathedral) did not. He was well supplied, however, with Canadian conscientiousness. Bishop Gray in his office, referring to a perfectly healthy clergyman of indecisive character, remarked to Mr. Franks, "Mr. X has had his spinal column removed." The Canadian, who may not have heard of the slang "backbone," said, "I must go call on him. What hospital?"

Bishop John M. Allin '43 to ABC, March, 1978.

F. D. R.

WHEN FRANKLIN D. ROOSEVELT was elected president in 1932, there hadn't been an Episcopalian in the White House since his cousin Theodore. Sewanee hoped to be the first college to award him an honorary degree. Admiral Cary T. Grayson '03, president of the American Red Cross, was asked to arrange an appointment.

The President soon received a formal visit from the Chancellor, Bishop Gailor, Vice-Chancellor Benjamin F. Finney, and the secretary of the board of regents, Charles Edward Thomas. It was a memorable occasion with two of the most formidable raconteurs in the country telling each other one story after another. The President thanked his visitors for their proffered honor and said, "I will be glad to accept if the 1933 session of Congress has adjourned in time for Commencement." All was made ready because not in years had Congress stayed in session much past May 1. This, however, turned out to be the Congress before which Roosevelt unveiled his then-radical proposals for economic recovery, and a few days before graduation it was clear that the President would not be on hand. Roosevelt suggested to Bishop Gailor that his new Postmaster General, Jim Farley, who had never attended college, receive the degree instead.

Charles Edward Thomas '27 to ABC, sometime in 1948.

POLITICALLY INSPIRED

DR. OSCAR TORIAN was a trustee of the University of the South at the time Franklin D. Roosevelt declined his honorary degree. It was represented to the board that Jim Farley had been told that he would receive the doctorate from the University of the South. The ordinances prescribed a unanimous vote for an honorary degree awarded under such circumstances. With Jim Farley actually on the way to Sewanee, there were grumblings of dissent. Bishop Reese was called on to mastermind the undercover work which had to be done to avoid a very embarrassing situation.

Bishop Gailor was presiding. He appointed Henry T. Soaper '94 and

130

the Reverend "Pop" McGlohon '81 as tellers. After the vote (following many speeches), Soaper rose to announce the result. He said, "There are forty-seven ballots marked YES, and one ballot which is illegible." The lone trustee who had voted in the negative did not make himself known. The unanimous vote was recorded, and Jim Farley received his honorary degree.

O. N. Torian '96 to ABC, September 2, 1961.

B.A.M. ON FARLEY

Dear Arthur:

I was a member of the Board of Trustees when Jim Farley was voted an honorary degree. . . . There was a rule that if a candidate were presented for an honorary degree at any time less than 90 days from Commencement, the vote would have to be unanimous. . . . There were speeches approving the award, and none of them gave any satisfactory reason why Jim Farley should be awarded an honorary degree by Sewanee other than it would please the President. . . . Henry Soaper from Kentucky was in charge of collecting and counting the ballots. I wrote a distinct "No" on my ballot. Henry . . . returned with the statement that all of the ballots were in the affirmative but one, and he could not read that ballot. . . . I think it was [Tennessee Justice] Arthur Crownover [who] moved that since one of the votes was illegible, the degree be awarded, and this motion was seconded and carried with a whoop by everyone but me, which apparently went unnoticed at the time. . . . You are free to use this in your anecdotes if you so desire.

B. Allston Moore '23 to ABC, February 28, 1962. *Note from Alumni Secretary: Alumnus Farley for many years never failed to send an annual gift to his adopted alma mater.*

NO RED TAPE

J OURNALIST AND BUSINESSMAN Robert Gibson wrote a letter to Bishop Henry St. George Tucker saying that he was "thinking about studying for the ministry." Bishop Tucker wrote back, "I accept your application as postulant and have entered you at Virginia Seminary."

Bishop Robert F. Gibson to ABC, March, 1978.

T HE DEAN was at his St. Luke's Hall desk in Sewanee in 1949 when a telephone call came from the Rev. Dr. Zabriskie saying that he had been elected Suffragan Bishop of Virginia. Gibson exclaimed, "O my God!" His secretary said, "Who died?"

Bishop Gibson to ABC, March, 1978. *Robert F. Gibson accepted, to the incredulity of his Sewanee friends, who muttered, "Why would a Dean at Sewanee leave to be a mere Bishop?"*

CLIFFHANGER

G ETTING CONSECRATED was not easy for Suffragan-Bishop-Elect Robert F. Gibson in 1949. The time and place had been announced, guests invited, and principals assembled at Alexandria. Bishop Frederick Goodwin was a bit sticky about letters dimissory from "foreign" jurisdictions such as Tennessee. He had to have one. Bishop Edmund Pendleton Dandridge of Tennessee had some canonical clauses to support a thesis that he could not with propriety give a transfer to a priest who had served, not his diocese, but the School of Theology at Sewanee—owned by many dioceses. The organ prelude had begun, the congregation seated, the procession formed, when Bishop Goodwin announced there would be no consecration unless there was a letter of transfer from Bishop Dandridge, standing at his elbow. In a rare defeat, the Lord Bishop of Tennessee (later Dean of the Seminary at Sewanee) pulled from his inside coat pocket a used envelope, scratched on it a note of transfer, handed it to Bishop Goodwin, and the ceremonials proceeded.

Bishop Robert F. Gibson to ABC, March, 1978.

SOUND PREJUDICE

W HEN JACK ALLIN was a young postulant from Arkansas, Bishop R. Bland Mitchell '08 asked to be driven to Petit Jean Mountain, where the diocesan summer camp was later named for him. They stopped for lunch at a roadside cafeteria, and both selected a dish which looked like strip steak. Allin tasted it and said, "Excellent liver." Bishop Mitchell, without tasting, called the waitress and said, "I can't eat this." She was quite flustered, but he made no explanation. Turn-inn to Jack, he said, "I have never been able to eat liver, not since the ptomaine poisoning at Magnolia Hall at Sewanee." Jack inquired, "Did you get sick?" "No," the Bishop said. "In fact, it was finally determined that the students were sick because of tainted milk and not because of the liver."

John M. Allin '43 to ABC, March 17, 1978. *The editor would observe that good sound prejudice is not invariably logical.*

NO FRILLS FARE

T HE PRESIDING BISHOP in 1977 was visiting Japan. There was a great ceremony at Rikkyo University in which Bishop Allin received an honorary degree, in the company of Primates, Archbishops, Metropolitans, and others. Afterward, photographers gathered, and Bishop Allin was asked to pose before a bust of the late Henry St. George Tucker, Bishop of Virginia before becoming Presiding Bishop, but before *that* a missionary to Japan and president of St. Paul's College, Tokyo, which evolved into Rikkyo. Bishop Allin, sizing up the situation, removed his ceremonial cope and mitre. "Bishop Tucker would not approve." he said. "It was not so much a matter of churchmanship with him but just the innate simplicity and humility of the man." The photo was shot that way. No frills.

Bishop John M. Allin '43 to ABC, March, 1978.

CHAPTER SIX

BENEFACTORS

In Memoriam
Frances T. D. Taylor
Baltimore

First to Bequeath a Legacy to
The University of the South
1870

"And she a Stranger"

The Historiographer is still hoping, at the time of editing this book, that something can be found about the life of this early benefactor.

GHOST OF MORGAN'S STEEP

T HE FIRST legend I heard as a freshman in 1932 was about General Morgan jumping his horse off Morgan's Steep. It was probably the best-established tale of the Mountain, the one everybody heard. When I learned twenty years later it wasn't true, it was as traumatic as finding out about Santa Claus.

The first clue came when I read in a reprint of early University papers a reference to "our benefactor Judge O. J. Morgan." Then I came upon a map of Sewanee, drawn in 1859, which named Morgan's Steep. Why, one might inquire, would a view be named for a general before he was a general to commemorate a deed before it was done? I had meantime established the fact that General John Hunt Morgan, the great cavalry raider who went into Indiana during The War, had actually died in Greeneville, Tennessee, clad in his nightshirt, shot by perfidious Yankees who did not understand romance. This did not clinch the case, for Morgan might have jumped off Morgan's Steep during the withdrawal of 1863 and still lived, as claimed by Ned Green. Obviously more was needed. Finally it arrived.

Browsing through the *Washington* (D. C.) *Intelligencer* of September 13, 1859, I found this item:

> Hon. Oliver J. Morgan, of Carroll Parish, Louisiana, who is now spending his third summer at Beersheba Springs, on Saturday, August 20th, gave Bishop Polk the large sum of forty thousand dollars to establish a Professorship of Agricultural Chemistry in the University of the South. This truly munificent donation completes the subscription required by the charter, five hundred thousand dollars, though the trustees have no idea of stopping there.

The necessity of laying to rest Sewanee's most persistent ghost became urgent with the publication of another in the long line of re·prints of this Morgan myth. On page 105 of *Ely* (an autobiography by Elisha Green, Seabury Press, 1966), the Sewanee-born black who assisted Willie Six attributes this to his grandfather, Ned Green, the garbage man and privy cleaner of the campus: "Grandpa told me that General Morgan had jumped off that rock. His horse was killed but the general got away. He said, 'The Yankees almost caught him. He and his bushwhackers gave them Yankees hell around these canyons That rock is named after him.' "

The testimony of Grandpa Ned Green is hard to confute, but all it actually proves is that he heard a memorable story in Sewanee's very earliest days.

'Tis time we honored a significant benefactor—Judge Oliver J. Morgan—who had nothing to do with the ghost of a Confederate raider.

ABC, from assorted notes and edited from *Sewanee News,* February, 1964.

HODGSON LIBRARY

J AMES POTTER, father of Mrs. Telfair Hodgson, Sr., pledged to Bishop Stephen Elliott before the War a gift for the University of the South. Sherman's march destroyed his estate, Potter died, and his son was killed by a sniper in Atlanta. Recovering some income from the land and shepherding some northern securities, the astute Rev. Telfair Hodgson made a series of wise investments and while serving as rector of a parish in Hoboken, decided with his wife that her father's pledge should be made good. They gave Sewanee its first stone building, a $10,000 library. In 1874 that was the largest gift which had come to the University. In 1878 Hodgson was elected first dean of the seminary and the following year became third Vice-Chancellor.

ABC, *Sewanee Alumni News,* February, 1955. *The stone library proved too far from the center of the campus, and the building became the nucleus of Emerald-Hodgson Hospital. In 1976 the structure on that site became a dormitory, Hodgson Hall.*

SOLICITOR

M AXIMILIAN BETHUNE WELLBORN moved from Eufaula, Alabama, to southwestern Arkansas in 1859. He bought for $20,000 a plantation near the Red River from a Mrs. Pickett who lived in Shreveport. When he went to deliver the cash, Bishop Polk was there, and she handed him $5,000 as a contribution to the University of the South.

Arthur Wellborn (son of M.B.W.) to ABC, April 18, 1957.

CHARLOTTE MORRIS MANIGAULT

Mrs. Henry M. Manigault [is] the daughter of the late Lewis Morris of Morrisiana, New York, who married a Miss Elliott of South Carolina and had large estates in the South, dying during the Confederate War on his plantation. His son, Captain Manigault Morris, was Commander of the Confederate steamer Florida, and his sister, Mrs. Manigault, has resided in England since the war. She has endowed two scholarships and the Trustees have themselves established a scholarship to be known as the Henry Manigault Scholarship, the Bishop of South Carolina having *in perpetua* the nomination.

Clipping from Nashville *American* in Charles Todd Quintard Diary, October 18, 1876.

MANIGAULT FAMILY

The Manigaults had the status in South Carolina that the Carters had in Virginia. The founder of the fortune was Gabriel Manigault, son of a Huguenot immigrant, who when he died in 1781 was the richest man in the Commonwealth. His plantation "Silk Hope" on the Cooper River went to his grandson Gabriel who owned 210 slaves in 1790. The plantation then passed to a brother-in-law Nathaniel Heyward who had 2,087 slaves in 1850. His daughter married Charles Manigault.

Ulrich B. Phillips, *Life and Labor in the Old South*, p. 255. *There are few names more significant than Manigault in the University's early history.*

DECISION

A T BRIGHTON I found Capt. C. Manigault Morris, ye commander of ye Confederate steamer Florida. He has been residing here with his family for five years past. His sister Mrs. Manigault also resides here & I had a delightful visit with them. . . . May 22. Went to Mrs. Manigault's for luncheon. Mrs. M. is a widow of independent means & has purchased ye house in which she resides. We talked over ye University of ye South and before I left she gave me a cheque for $100 on her New York Banker Henry Meigs, Esq. & promised to endow a Scholarship as a memorial of her husband. . . . May 29. Mrs. Manigault met us at luncheon (in Brighton) & after that I returned with her to her residence & had a *long* talk about ye University of ye South. She decided to give me two Scholarships of 1,000 pounds each, to be paid in two years. In ye evening I had another conference with her & proposed to her ye building of ye Theological Hall. I told her not to make up her mind hastily but that we would go to ye Holy Communion at 8 o'clock in the morning & then & there she would decide. The next morning we were early at St. Paul's Church. After ye service I walked home with her and to my *unspeakable joy* she placed in my hand an order on her bankers in New York for ye sum of $14,000. . . . At ye same time she informed me that she should leave an endowment for a Scholarship by her will of $5,000. . . . Then she said, "I am indebted to you for helping me come to a conclusion in this matter & as you were once a physician I should like ye hall named St. Luke's." Ye Scholarship, a Memorial of her husband, is to be named St. Andrew's, Mr. Manigault having died on St. Andrew's Day. This is such a blessed consummation of all my hopes & such a crown to all my labors that I concluded to send a dispatch by cable to Genl. Gorgas announcing ye fact. . . . "A Memorial Theological Hall is provided for."

Charles Todd Quintard Diary, May 20, 1876, *et. seq. Despite repeated invitations, Mrs. Manigault never visited Sewanee, but the Bishop saw her on each of his last two trips to England and kept in touch by correspondence. She continued to contribute, and at her death in 1901 there had come to the University some of the library's most valuable volumes in addition to vestments of museum quality and her personal jewelry.*

BILLION DOLLAR BELL

T HOMPSON UNION, replaced by the Bishop's Common as hub of student activity, was first called the Chemical and Philosophical Hall. It was the site of the Medical Department from 1892 to 1909. Later its upstairs auditorium, once a dissecting room for anatomy classes, became the theatre, used for movies and for Purple Masque productions. The first floor became the home of the Sewanee Union with rooms furnished elegantly by Mrs. James L. Houghteling, widow of the founder of the Brotherhood of St. Andrew. At the time of its destruction by fire in 1950, the sandwich shop, student post office, and lounge occupied the first floor.

Jacob Thompson was born at Leasburg, Caswell County, North Carolina, on May 15, 1810. He was the third son of well-to-do Lucretia Van Hook Thompson and Nicholas Thompson, a prosperous tanner. He graduated with honors from the University at Chapel Hill in 1831 and remained eighteen months as a tutor. Over the protests of his father, who wanted him to be a minister, Thompson studied law in Greensboro and was admitted to the North Carolina bar in 1835.

Jacob's brother James Young, a physician, had gone to the New Southwest and when the land office opened at Pontotoc following the cession of the Chickasaw tract, the brothers settled there. Jacob organized courts of law in each of the ten new counties, was elected to the Mississippi legislature, and in 1839 was elected to the United States Congress. On a trip back to the Delta between sessions, the handsome young statesman met Miss Catherine Jones, called the most beautiful girl in the Mississippi Valley. She was also one of the wealthiest.

After the custom of the time, Jacob presented himself to her father, asking for Miss Catherine's hand. There was a disparity in their ages, Thompson being about twice as old as the young lady. Furthermore, Paton Jones pointed out that he wanted his daughter to receive an education. The ingenious Thompson, knowing that he dare not go unbetrothed back to Washington lest some young blade steal his lady, made this interesting proposal. He, Thompson, would marry Catherine and would take her direct to a convent in France where she would complete her education. When she was eighteen, they would set up housekeeping. Ardor won the day, and all went according to agreement. Vivacious and voluptuous, Catherine Thompson became an ideal planter's wife and a celebrated Washington hostess.

In 1855 Thompson had been persuaded to accept nomination to the United States Senate, but he withdrew in favor of a less well-known political aspirant, Jefferson Davis. In 1857 Thompson became Secretary of the Interior under James Buchanan. He remained in the cabinet until January, 1861, when the *Star of the West* was ordered to Fort Sumter. He returned to Mississippi to aid in organizing Confederate troops, numerous companies of which were equipped from his private funds.

Thompson had positions of great responsibility and danger in the war. He served as aide to Beauregard at Shiloh. He was present throughout the siege of Vicksburg. In 1863 he was called to Richmond and asked by President Davis to direct the hazardous Confederate spy activities in Canada. Thereafter every bonfire north of the Mason-Dixon line was blamed on him. When the war was over the price on his head was $100,000, according to a printed handbill pasted in the diary of Bishop Charles T. Quintard.

Before the end of the war there took place the remarkable journey by Mrs. Thompson which is intimately connected with the subsequent building of Thompson Hall. For a large fee (one source says $5,000), a Canadian girl delivered to Mrs. Thompson in Mississippi a message that her husband was not dead, as had been reported, but that he wanted her to bury the silver, come through Federal lines to meet him in Canada, and bring with her only one piece of paper, a receipt for £200,000 in British stocks, investments he had been making over a period of years from their cotton profits.

With forged papers, Mrs. Thompson started up the Mississsippi by packet steamer. At Memphis she was sent ashore with other passengers and, behind a screen with a lady attendant, she was stripped to the skin. When her corset, into which she had sewn the slip of paper, was handed to inspecting guards, she told a joke. It must have been good, for the soldiers tossed the garment back over the screen, and she was allowed to continue her flight.

There was one more inspection point to be passed at Cairo, Illinois. For this ordeal the clever Catherine Thompson was ready. In Germany after a skiing accident she had acquired a partial upper dental plate. Wadding the receipt, she put it in the roof of her mouth and went safely through to be reunited with her husband. Escape abroad was the next consideration. They decided to go through Maine to Nova Scotia and thence to England. Unknown to Thompson, his minutest movements were being reported to President Lincoln from the moment he left Canada. According to Carl Sandburg, agents waited while repeated telegrams to Lincoln asked for orders to capture the prize prisoner. For reasons best understood in the gentle consciousness of that great man, Lincoln allowed Thompson to sail without even knowing of his danger. A potentially perfect scapegoat was allowed to live to serve the Episcopal Church and Sewanee.

In 1868 the Thompsons returned to Mississippi, vastly wealthy by comparison with neighbors and friends. They decided to settle in Memphis. Thompson became a vestryman of Calvary Church, a delegate to diocesan and general conventions, a principal personal benefactor to Jefferson Davis, and in 1873 a member of the board of trustees of the University of the South. For twelve years he was one of the three-man Executive Committee which corresponded to the present board of regents. When it became necessary to mortgage the buildings and lands of the University, Thompson with Albert T. McNeal purchased a third of the $40,000 worth of bonds.

By 1880 Sewanee appeared to be recovering under the firm vice-chancellorship of the Rev. Telfair Hodgson. There were only two stone buildings, the Hodgson Library (later Emerald-Hodgson Hospital) and St. Luke's Hall. Thompson urged the trustees to build "Chemical and Philosophical Hall" toward which he made the largest single contribution, $1,000. A little over a year after its completion in 1883, he died, and his will had this interesting codicil.

"I own $100,000 in the *Bell Telephone Company* stock, at Washington City. I request my wife to transfer this stock to the *Trustees of the University of the South*. . . . Should the stock not be valuable . . . I request her to turn over to the University $10,000."

In a letter dated June 14, 1885, Mrs. Thompson asked the pleasure of the trustees. Did they want the telephone stock or the $10,000 in cash?

On August 5, 1885, Albert T. McNeal, reporting for the Finance Committee of the board of trustees (see page 43 of the *Proceedings* of that year), said, "In regard to the legacy of the Hon. Jacob Thompson . . . we recommend that the board . . . receive $10,000 in cash in

141

full of said legacy rather than rely upon the possibilities of the Telephone Stock."

ABC. *It is the fate of trustees—and boards thereof—to deviate from perfection. But when the Sewanee board of 1885 erred, it erred colossally. And if Jacob Thompson is not listed with such benefactors to education as John Harvard, John D. Rockefeller, Paul Tulane, and Leland Stanford, it is not his fault. He tried.*

HUNDRED-AND-FIFTY WHAT?

O<small>N</small> D<small>ECEMBER</small> 5, 1911, the Sewanee alumni gave a dinner at the University Club in New York City. At my request Mr J. Pierpont Morgan attended the dinner, and was quite pleased with the pictures which were thrown upon a screen. Just as he was leaving, Mr. Morgan said to me, "I will give you one hundred and fifty to start your fund." And I said, "Do you mean one hundred and fifty thousand?" He said, "Yes, of course.'"

Next morning I went to the Library (of the Club) and saw Mr. Morgan and I asked him whether he would give me in writing that promise of $150,000. He said to me: "Have I ever failed you?" This was the last time I ever saw him. He died not long afterwards, and the University never got that $150,000. He was a noble and kindly gentleman, and I thank God upon every remembrance of him.

Edited from Bishop Thomas Frank Gailor, *Some Memories* (Kingsport: Southern Publishers, 1937), page 140.

BIRTHSTONE

W<small>ILLIAM</small> S<small>TERLING</small> C<small>LAIBORNE</small> '00, Rector of Otey and Commissary of the University, besides raising money for St. Mary's and St. Andrew's schools, worked for the hospital. He got the elder Mrs. Hodgson to let him have the use of a building she had given which was standing idle. When it burned, he went north and got the money for the new hospital from Mrs. Schermerhorn Auchmuty, who gave it as a memorial to friends who had been born in May, and whose birthstone was the emerald. She asked that the hospital be named Emerald in honor of her friends. Mrs. Auchmuty continued to give to the hospital her entire life. Indeed, Mrs. Claiborne recorded that a Philadelphia lady had once asked her husband, "Who will carry on your work when you are gone?" Mr. Claiborne replied, "My friends will carry on my work." "When," Mrs. Claiborne continued, "I put this in a letter to Mrs. Auchmuty, by return mail I got a check for $30,000 to endow a bed at the hospital. This shows how the friends he made loved him."

Minnie M. Claiborne to ABC, November 14, 1953.

SAVINGS ACCOUNT

In 1924 Bishop Theodore DuBose Bratton '82 conducted a preaching mission at Christ Church, Mobile. A young woman sitting on the crowded chancel steps underwent a profound spiritual experience which changed her life. She began a correspondence with Bishop Bratton which continued as long as he lived and made the church's work her central focus. In 1929 she responded to his appeal, published in the diocesan paper, for funds to help extend domestic missions, with the suggestion that she might begin a fund which would ultimately support that work. The Bishop replied, "Much as I need the money, I urge you instead to establish a memorial fund at the University of the South."

Olive Miriam Moss was born in Jubilee, Illinois, October 13, 1891. Her grandparents, who came west via the new canal from Onondaga, New York, had been associated with Bishop Philander Chase in establishing Jubilee College in 1837. Olive's parents moved here and there seeking a better climate for her father, but by 1918 she had settled independently in Mobile and begun her lifelong employment as a postal clerk.

With Olive Moss, the Bishop's suggestion was a command. She opened a savings account, placing in it $12 each month from her $85 salary. She never inherited from relatives, and she never made more than $200 per month, but when she died in 1970, leaving everything to the University, the total estate came to $12,112 which was placed, according to her wishes, in the endowment fund of the theological school in memory of her stepmother.

ABC, executor of her estate, Treasurer's records.

BISHOP'S COMMON CORNER

THE SITE selected for the Bishop's Common at the corner of Alabama and Georgia Avenues is near that of old Miller Hall. Miss Mary Miller, who died in 1916 at the age of seventy, was the daughter of a British naval officer and a Chinese lady of rank. When her mother died in China her father brought her to Nashville to be reared by an aunt. This lady was very jealous of the girl, and, when Mary fell in love with a clergyman, the aunt intimated that her niece was illegitimate. Stung by shame, Mary declined to marry the priest. Years later, after the aunt's death, she found papers which established her legitimacy even by Western standards.

Miss Miller moved to Sewanee, remaining until her death. For many years she kept one of the loveliest of the summer boarding houses and halls for students. In her will she left money for the cemetery, a codicil for the Byrd Douglas scholarship, and her property to the University. The arched gateway over the footpath at the northwest corner of the cemetery was built in her memory. Her home was later occupied by Gen. James Postell Jervey, John Hodges '34, and William W. Lewis '04.

David A. Shepherd '00 to ABC, June 3, 1952.

WILDERNESS

WHEN DR. WILLIAM MECKLENBURG POLK came to Sewanee to make an address about 1914, his wife, knowing she was leaving New York for the unsettled frontier, brought along a tin bathtub and a mattress. The visitors stayed with the Cleveland K. Benedicts, where Sewanee's best foot was always forward and where it was hoped that the wealthy son of Bishop Polk might become a benefactor to his father's favorite cause. To the consternation of all, Dr. Polk fell down the Benedict steps and broke a rib. It was his last trip to Sewanee, and they didn't even leave the bathtub.

Samuel Benedict '20 to ABC, February, 1961.

144

RECTIFIED

D<small>R</small>. W<small>ILLIAM</small> E<small>GLESTON</small> '94 spent ten years at Sewanee in Grammar School, College, and Medical Department, probably influenced by his cousin Miss Maria Porcher who built Magnolia Hall. He practiced in Hartsville, South Carolina, served repeatedly as trustee, and died on March 24, 1935, meantime having sent both sons to the University. He was a generous man during his lifetime and what with the inroads of the depression he did not have enough cash in his estate to pay the $10,000 he had specified for Sewanee in his will. Members of his family remedied the matter over a period of years by establishing two scholarship funds in his name, one in the college and one in the seminary.

Dr. DuBose Egleston '33 to ABC, November, 1972.

BRUNING BROTHERS

C<small>HARLES</small> E. B<small>RUNING</small> was 32 years old when he received his M.D. from the medical school at Sewanee in 1895. He practiced in New Orleans all his life and died in 1950. His obituary came through the clipping service and indicated that he was survived by his brother Theodore George Bruning. A fire had recently destroyed the student union which earlier had been the medical building where Bruning had labored as a student. I wrote a letter to Theodore asking if he would like to make a memorial gift from his brother's estate to restore the building at a cost of $75,000. There was no reply, but in 1953 a letter from Bruning's attorney brought a copy of Theodore's will. Sure enough, the codicil was there—$75,000 to the University of the South in memory of Charles in gratitude for his medical training at Sewanee. The bronze tablet recording the gift belongs in the Jacob Thompson building.

ABC, Bruning file in Archives, and notes.

HONORS

I N THE early 1940's Bishop McKinstry, who had become a close friend and counselor to Jessie Ball duPont, noticed that she was not in *Who's Who*. Having himself been in its pages since he was thirty-five years old, he wrote a note to the editor inquiring if she shouldn't be listed. The editor sent word, "Give us more information about her." With the secret help of her secretary, the Bishop compiled a formidable dossier. Mrs. duPont was in the next edition and was highly pleased. Soon afterward the Bishop, who was already receiving aid for several young people each year from her college scholarship program, observed that here was a woman doing wonderful work for education and yet no college had offered her an honorary degree. He phoned Dr. Alexander Guerry, who said, "Nominate her and send a supporting letter." Bishop McKinstry used the *Who's Who* material and, when the degree was voted, he and Mrs. McK. accompanied her on the train to Chattanooga. Bishop and Mrs. Juhan entertained the whole party at their Sewanee home. Next year Washington and Lee gave her a second honorary degree.

Bishop Arthur R. McKinstry to ABC, March 13, 1974.

AMERICAN AUTHOR

T HE MOST beautiful and sensitive bit of prose ever written about Sewanee was by William Alexander Percy '04 in his autobiography *Lanterns on the Levee*. Percy was on the faculty too briefly in 1908-09 and 1919-20. He served as trustee in 1922. In Greenville, Mississippi, he managed family properties, practiced law, and wrote some poetry and prose still cherished by lucky readers who discover his works. When he died in 1942 at the age of fifty-six, he left his modest estate to his three nephews but also remembered Sewanee with a gift of $2,500 to be used "for purchase of books by American authors." Each year the income is used for that purpose, and his personal bookplate decorates the inside front cover.

ABC, Archives file on Percy and notes.

NO ROOM

U p to 1967, the largest bequest in the history of the University was that of George Reynolds Parker (1870-1930) which came to $1,506,960. It was specified as a memorial to his mother, English-born Mary Elizabeth Green Parker, and his wife Virginia Harvison who like himself was born in Louisville. He was a successful tobacco merchant who in 1920 devoted himself to investments as an associate of the Security Trust Company of Lexington. Through the influence of his fellow Episcopalian Henry T. Soaper, Parker was elected to the board of trustees of the University and then to the board of regents. At his death, half of his estate was placed in trust for relatives with the University as legatee after the expiration of life interests. The other half of his estate went without restriction to his wife. In May 1947 Mrs. Parker made a trip, unannounced, to Sewanee for the presumed purpose of determining whether or not she would bequeath her half of the estate to the University, as her husband had done. Unhappily there was no room at the Inn (Tuckaway), and she left unimpressed, dying shortly thereafter.

ABC, Archives files on Henry T. Soaper, George R. Parker.

A memorial minute described Parker as "frail, dynamic, with keen and searching wit, intellectually honest, widely informed, devoted to friends, loyal to every duty, sympathetic to those who suffered, enthusiastic for the young—a life spent in doing good."

WILKINS SCHOLARSHIPS

A momentous turning point in the history of the University of the South came when, through the influence of Malcolm Fooshee, the George F. Baker Trust of New York made a series of three grants of $50,000 each to enable Sewanee to attract about a half-dozen students a year who were especially bright. When the last of these grants was expiring, there developed, providentially, the interest of a lady in Warm Springs, Georgia, in scholarship aid at Sewanee.

Miss Georgia Mustian Wilkins died June 20, 1959, at the age of 77. She was small, nimble, alert, generous, and the possessor of a keen sense of humor. Among her close friends were next-door-neighbors Franklin and Eleanor Roosevelt. She left a remarkable will, a veritable catalogue of the charitable works which had occupied her life. She provided roughly $100,000 for friends, $300,000 to a score of causes, and the remainder, nearly $2,000,000—she divided between her church and Sewanee.

Since her special interest had always been in scholarship aid for students, it was decided to create a permanent fund, perpetuating the Baker Scholar concept, by which Wilkins Scholars would be enabled to attend the University and provide an academic elite. If it is true that students learn as much from their peers as from teachers, then it follows that intellectual leadership among students is in a category of importance with gifted faculty.

ABC, notes and recollections.

PALFREY FUND

WILLIAM TAYLOR PALFREY was born February 24, 1866, in New Iberia, Louisiana, and died at the age of 94 in Houston with the Very Rev. J. Milton Richardson, later bishop, conducting the service at the Cathedral. Apparently Mr. Palfrey first heard about Sewanee in the 1880's when some of his cousins attended. For over a half century there is no record of correspondence with him, but in October, 1950, he visited Sewanee. He subsequently asked to be put on the mailing list and from then until his death in 1960, writing first from Denver and then from Houston, he kept up a stream of letters, most of them enclosing clippings of interest to the alumni office. For quite a while there was confusion over his identity because another William Taylor Palfrey, also from Louisiana, had attended Sewanee briefly at the time of World War I. When finally the family was "straightened out" by Mr. Palfrey, he began sending names and addresses of people who might help the University. He was very clear throughout his correspondence that he wanted all he had to come to Sewanee. Dean Richardson became well acquainted with the lonely gentleman and on one occasion was embarrassed when a new parish secretary, noting his well-worn clothing, thought he had come to the Cathedral to ask for a meal. The Palfrey estate came to $87,035, and its income has been used regularly for student aid.

William T. Palfrey to ABC, letters through the 1950's.

ASHES

The Cumberland Forest Festival, predecessor of the Sewanee Summer Music Center, opened an entirely new vein of Sewanee enthusiasts. Prior to that first series of summer concerts in 1950 Sewanee's forays into the world of serious music had been largely via the Chapel choir, the organ, occasional piano concerts, and string groups.

Among new people attracted to the Mountain by classical music was Judge Ellett N. Shepherd of Denver. He came to the first concerts of Roy and Johana Harris and continued to come every summer that his frail health permitted. Sometimes he stayed with the Chitties, sometimes with the David Shepherds, with whom he was never able to trace a kinship.

For Judge Shepherd, the University of the South became a consuming interest. He personally built the first modern Hi-Fi record-playing system the University owned. He decided to place Sewanee in his will, explaining that, due to probable hospitalization, the estate might not be very large. We talked about it and corresponded about it. By the time of his death February 28, 1965, we had become close friends.

When his will was probated, sure enough the University was principal beneficiary, he having had no family. He had asked his executor to have his remains cremated and sent to me. I would know what to do.

I thought about the matter, considering among other possibilities Green's View, which he loved so well. I finally decided to scatter some of the ashes there and to bury the remainder among the roots of the beautiful blue spruce tree at the northwest corner of the duPont Library yard. Ellett loved books, and he also loved the architecture of the little Hodgson Chapel across the street.

ABC, Archives file on Shepherd, and notes.

OVERSUBSCRIBED

Wᴴᴱɴ Dʀ. Oꜱᴄᴀʀ N. Tᴏʀɪᴀɴ started his pediatric wing at Sewanee, he asked his friends Eli and Josiah K. Lilly of Indianapolis for a gift of $5,000 which the Doctor thought would complete it. When he found that the wing would cost much more than that, he wrote his benefactors that at nearly eighty he did not think he should start so large a project and he was going to return their money. They wrote back and told him to keep the $5,000 and to let them know what the total cost would be. There were many delays with post-WWII shortages, and it was several months before he could get a firm estimate. Meantime his friends in Indianapolis wrote him regularly asking that he name the price. When he finally gave them the total—$14,000—they sent him $18,000.

Another story about Dr. Torian's relationship with the remarkable Lilly family also involves the amount of $5,000. A couple of years after the pediatric wing had been established as an adjunct to the Emerald-Hodgson Hospital, he needed more money. He wrote the Lilly Endowment and asked for $5,000. At the same time, he also wrote Josiah Kirby Lilly, Jr., and told "J. K." of his need for $5,000. Dr. Torian promptly received a check for that amount from the Endowment, and before he could thank its executive director, he received a similar check from Mr. J. K. Lilly. The doctor wrote his best letter of thanks to both and returned Mr. Lilly's check. In the next mail the check came back again to Sewanee with a note saying, "It was all a mistake, but since the mistake has been made, just keep the second check too."

O. N. Torian '96 to ABC, November 21, 1963.

The great pharmaceutical house of Indiana was founded by "Old Eli" who had served in the Civil War in Wilder's federal cavalry. His son Josiah Kirby Lilly came into the business with him, but it was Eli's grandsons under whose astute management the firm became one of the largest businesses of its kind in the world. Dr. Torian, one of the nation's pioneer pediatricians, treated three generations of Lilly children. The Lillys never forgot his devotion to their young.

INDIRECT BENEFIT

The largest bequest in the history of the University up to 1930 came from a man who never saw Sewanee and who did not know it would be his beneficiary. Edward Disney Farmer was born in England, moved to Vancouver, to Colorado, and then to Fort Worth. He brought some money with him and invested in downtown property. His old buddy from early days in the Southwest was George Beggs, an Episcopalian and a friend of a young lawyer named G. Bowdoin Craighill '03. Farmer wanted to leave his money to good causes but couldn't decide which ones. He left the estate to Beggs with instructions to dispose of it "to charitable and worthwhile purposes." Beggs, who also had never seen Sewanee, sought Craighill's advice, heard about the church's educational center in distant Tennessee, and created the Edward Disney Farmer Fund—$250,000—still producing income in the University's endowment portfolio. The oldest of the Sewanee lakes, located on the Brakefield Road is *not* "The Farm Pond" but, by action of the Regents, "The Farmer Pond."

ABC, from Archives files. *George Beggs III confirmed his father's association with E. D. Farmer, adding that Farmer died at Mayo Brothers hospital in Minnesota May 29, 1924.*

RIGHT AND WRONG

Lizzie Baker Bransford of Augusta, Georgia, left her entire estate in 1940 to the University of the South—almost $300,000. When her property and possessions were sold, there was left an elderly, seven-passenger, Packard limousine. The Sewanee Volunteer Fire Department at the time consisted of two or three lengths of garden hose mounted on a reel slung between bicycle wheels. Someone hatched the ingenious idea of converting the Bransford chassis into a fire engine. This was done, but trouble developed in the steering system which defied the best efforts of Sewanee's mechanics. The car would not make a right turn. Finally a solution was reached. The smoke-eating drivers learned to make a right turn by turning left, backing straight,

151

turning left, backing straight, and turning left again. For years the fine old machine never missed a fire though sometimes it was a mite late.

Oral testimony from contemporary members of SVFD—Sewanee Volunteer Fire Department—to ABC.

THE CLASS HAD CLASS

N o, SAID Bishop Juhan when I called on him that morning in 1957. "I have not heard from Mrs. Phillips." I was understandably concerned because ten days earlier the Bishop had sent a letter to Mrs. Frank P. Phillips of Columbus, Mississippi, a request for a gift of $75,000. The story was this.

Frank Phillips '93 had matriculated in 1887 at the old Sewanee Grammar School and in 1889 in the college. He had become a prosperous business man in Columbus, known for his generosity. During the 1940's he had vacationed at the Monteagle Assembly and on one occasion had been ill enough to be a patient at the Emerald-Hodgson Hospital in Sewanee where he was attended by his Sewanee contemporary Dr. Reynold Kirby-Smith '95, then chief of staff. When he died in 1949, the clipping service brought to the alumni office his obituary which revealed that, after some bequests to local charities, and $50,000 to Sewanee, his estate of about $500,000 had gone to his widow. About this time the Hill-Burton Act made available to hospitals matching grants for construction, dollar for dollar. The Sewanee hospital needed a residence for nurses and indeed had already borrowed the money for a $150,000 building toward which half would come from the government. The letter I drafted for Mrs. Phillips recalled her husband's happy days as a student, and from the alumni directory edited by my wife and Mrs. Petry, listed for Mrs. Phillips some of the men who had been at Sewanee with her husband—Bishops Troy Beatty of Tennessee, William T. Manning of New York, Henry J. Mikell of Atlanta, William Mercer Green, Jr. of Mississippi, Harry R. Carson of Haiti, C. B. Colmore of Puerto Rico, Campbell Gray of Northern Indiana and men who became founders or heads of banks, industrial enterprises, and businesses.

The letter asked if she would give the $75,000 needed to pay the

University's share for the nurses' home, in order that it might be Phillips Hall, a memorial to her husband. As I was about to leave the Bishop's study an unopened letter from the morning's mail dropped from his coat pocket. "Wait a minute, Arthur," he said as he slit the envelope. Sure enough, it was a handwritten note from Mrs. Phillips saying she would be happy to make the gift of $75,000 if the University would be willing to accept it in three annual installments. The University was willing.

ABC, from recollections and notes in Archives.

HIS CHURCH AND SEWANEE

Sewanee maintains permanent biographical archives on its benefactors as well as its alumni. The bequest of $5,000 from the late William Irvine Moody of Memphis brought to the files some remarkable facts about an interesting and generous citizen. Mr. Moody was in his 96th year when he died on May 15, 1960. He was descended from the Epps, Rawlings, Cocke, and Fry families of Georgia and Virginia. His father was a Confederate captain, receiving a wound near Chattanooga in 1864 from which he never recovered. The funeral service was said by Chaplain Charles T. Quintard, later Sewanee's first Vice-Chancellor. The boy born that same year back in LaGrange, Tennessee, became Sewanee's benefactor.

In Memphis, young "W.I." Moody, as he called himself, started to work for the Orgill Brothers hardware firm as billing clerk. He lived to become chairman of its board and to take part in much of the Episcopal Church's work in Memphis. He helped plan the Cathedral, helped organize the Memphis Chamber of Commerce, and raised money to pave Riverside Drive from Adams Street to Crump Boulevard. He left two daughters, three grandchildren, and seven great-grandchildren. He remembered "his church and Sewanee" in his will.

ABC, Archives file on Moody.

CROCKETT SCHOLARS

T HE NATHAN A. CROCKETT bequest was one of the University's largest. It was calculated in 1949 to be worth $385,000 but with the investments handled by the Third National Bank on behalf of the life interests, it had grown to $750,000 by 1970. Mr. Crockett was a Presbyterian, had not attended college, and never visited Sewanee. John A. Witherspoon '22, who worked nine years for Crockett, supplied these details. He was a big man, over six feet and weighing 230 pounds. He was local manager for Prudential Life until he became one of the founders of the Third National Bank and finally chairman of its board. When his first wife died he called vice-president Witherspoon to his desk and took him to the vault, showing him a box full of gilt-edge securities. Having no children, he wondered what he should do with the money. Witherspoon suggested an educational trust and in due course introduced Alexander Guerry to Crockett. They became good friends, and Guerry on trips to Nashville visited Crockett at the bank frequently. The trust as finally activated provides financial aid for students from Middle Tennessee with preference shown those from Giles County, where Crockett was a major stockholder of the Union Bank of Pulaski, his hometown.

John A. Witherspoon to ABC, February 25, 1974.

OUTDOORS

W HEN HE died of a sudden heart attack on June 10, 1965, at the age of forty-five, the Rev. James Young Perry, Jr., was the best known Episcopal priest among the young people of North Carolina. He had set his ministry in the outdoors on the theory that young people more readily establish a relationship with God in a natural setting. The vigor of his ministry so profoundly affected so many that on his death a memorial scholarship was begun with a fund of $27,874 from people of the diocese of Western North Carolina. Young Jim's father was a graduate of the class of '20, his mother was Annie Guerry, his grandfather was University Chaplain and Bishop, and his four Guerry uncles all alumni.

ABC, Archives folder on Perry, plus notes.

FROM THE MOUNTAINS OF SAVOIE

W HAT SOUNDS does the student associate with Sewanee? The first students undoubtedly carried away with them the memory of the pealing Meneely bell, hung with such affectionate care by General Josiah Gorgas in the little wooden tower at old St. Augustine's Chapel. Today's "Old Timers"—students of a half century ago—recall the Breslin chimes, ringing the quarter hours in the same tones as the Westminster chimes in London. But students of Sewanee's second century, not forgetting the perfect tone of the Meneely bell now in St. Luke's tower or the Breslin chimes—given in memory of Mrs. Charlotte Ferris Douglas in 1900—will remember best the range, the color, and variety of one of the world's great carillons.

The late W. Dudley Gale, III '20, remained for a time in France after World War I. There, besides a knowledge of the French language, drama, and art, he also acquired a love for the bells that pealed from little churches and big cathedrals. He acquired a technical knowledge of carillons when he, as chairman of the carillon committee of Christ Church, Nashville, spent weeks in consultation with America's great authority in the field, the late Dr. Arthur Lynds Bigelow of Princeton. And so it was natural that, when pondering a suitable centennial gift to the University in memory of his great-grandfather, Bishop-General Leonidas Polk, Gale thought of a carillon.

As conversations with Dr. Bigelow proceeded, Gale became more convinced that the Polk Carillon ought to be as nearly perfect as possible. The Princeton engineer made a special trip to Haute Savoie, near the French-Italian border, in the summer of 1955 to discuss details of the founding of the bells with the maker, Les Fils de Georges Paccard. Both Gale and Bigelow visited the foundry in 1957 for an inspection before the shipment left for New Orleans.

The carillon bell was first developed by the Flemish in the 1400's when polyphony was adding richness to the traditional melodies of religious music. For bells to sound together with pleasing effect, each must be near-perfect. The French Revolution and resultant economic distress stopped carillon making for a half century, and then the French were the first to return to the lost art. They are now considered world leaders in carillon-tuning.

The Polk Carillon which cost $65,000 constituted the second largest

155

gift to the All Saints' Chapel completion fund, the largest being that of the Shapard family of Griffin, Georgia after whom the tower is named. The set consists of 56 bells, three more than hang in world-famous Bok Tower at Lake Wales, Florida. The bass bells were installed in the lower belfry of Shapard Tower which had been redesigned to receive them. They were hung in place by a giant crane when the tower had been substantially completed but before the flooring at the top had been laid. The clavier in the tower has a duplicate practice keyboard in Woods Laboratories. An organist or pianist can learn how to play a carillon fairly readily, but there are still less than a hundred carillons in the entire country on which he can practice. Sewanee's set was the third largest in America when installed, and in 1972 was the ninth largest in number of bells. The range is a full four octaves, chromatic scale, plus a deep B-flat bourdon, plus five treble bells above the four octaves.

The largest bell weighing 7,500 pounds is called a swinging bourdon and is inscribed, "To Polk and to Sewanee, my Alma Mater, this carillon is dedicated." In bas-relief on the reverse is the University seal whose circular chain has a link for each of the 22 dioceses which then owned the University.

Seventeen of the other bells are also inscribed in a manner traditional in bell founding. They are memorials to members of the donor's family. Dudley Gale's father attended the Sewanee Grammar School in 1875 and was a long-time trustee of the University. The first William Dudley Gale served as aide to General Polk and married his daughter. George Gale '24 died in 1946.

Mrs. Gale, the former Evelyn Douglas, also had family ties with Sewanee. She died several years before her husband and her mother, Mrs. Douglas, who left the University a significant bequest. The major part of Gale's own estate came to the University, making the total benefaction from the family considerably more than a half million dollars. A bell honors Gale's mother, Meta Jackson Gale of Nashville.

Still another bell is for an apostle—"My name is Saint Luke, Patron of Sewanee. When I ring may all her sons harken to my voice." Another calls attention to its musical note: "From the Mountains of Savoie to the Mountains of Tennessee, I sing Sol." Another bell's inscription says in Latin: "No brazen voice, gathered into the circled bound, in any other field is found, to ring a song of sweeter sound." Still another bell is dedicated to Joan of Arc.

Dr. Bigelow considered the Polk Carillon his finest work and one of the most important instruments in the world, capable of playing any music composed for the carillon, able to express anything the bellmaster desires.

ABC, edited from *Sewanee Alumni News*, November, 1956.

TOWERED CITY

S EWANEE AS Gardiner Tucker's "towered city" became more plausible when Shapard Tower appeared in the 1950's as part of the completion of All Saints' Chapel. There had been Breslin, modeled on Magdalen Tower, Oxford, the Phi Delta Theta house inspired by Founders' Tower there, and the slim tower of St. Luke's Chapel. Chapel plans included a tower from the beginning by Silas McBee '78, through the successive designs of Ralph Adams Cram and Edward McCrady, who altered his tower to accommodate the Polk Carillon.

Shapard Tower is named for Robert Payne Shapard, textile manufacturer of Griffin, Georgia, whose son, grandsons and great-grandson studied at Sewanee. His wife "Precious" was a great lady who delighted in annual houseparties at the Monteagle Assembly.

The carillon is presided over by Albert Bonholzer, who learned to play the bells as a young church organist. Twenty-five years after the Coca-Cola business called him back to Tracy City, there sprang up nearby a magnificent instrument on which to teach his art to generations of Sewanee students.

Mary Elizabeth Bonholzer Baggenstoss to ENC, years ago, and affectionate memories of Mrs. R. P. Shapard.

157

CHAPTER SEVEN

LADIES

QUEENIE WOODS WASHINGTON

"Miss Queenie can tell you anything about early Sewanee." Her husband's cousin Maud Tompkins Kirby-Smith was only one of dozens who told me that as I began looking for the human side of Sewanee history in 1946. A heavy correspondence had already developed between Miss Queenie and me when I moved to Tulane for graduate work while I recovered from viral hepatitis in 1951.

For a year I saw her frequently, for a total of hundreds of hours, always in lace in a four-poster bed, beautiful even in her eighties. In the days before I had access to recording equipment, I painstakingly jotted notes which I later transcribed.

QUEENIE WOODS WASHINGTON deserves a full-length biography. The classic tragedy of her life makes high drama. She was born in Nashville, the center of a memorable society. She was beautiful and surpassingly intelligent, but her life was blighted. She loved—and was dearly loved by—a man she didn't marry. Instead she followed the implications of the curiously inadequate comment attributed to Robert E. Lee, "Duty is the noblest word. . . ." She was the youngest of a house full of sisters in a family reduced to post-Civil War poverty. She saw it as her duty to relieve the penury of the family. She did it— via the altar. She was a good wife, giving all that had been bargained for. In time her husband went to his reward.

Then and only then did she write a letter addressed to Mr. William B. Thompson '87, at the height of the 1920's a brilliant, successful, bachelor businessman of New Orleans. In it she merely told him of the death of her husband, reported where she was and what doing, expressed the hope that he was well. She waited expectantly, then incredulously. There was no reply. Months lengthened to years as she tried to put from her mind the crushing disappointment. He no longer loved her, and she knew that to be her just reward. With her sorrow complete, she read finally of his death and received from friends the endless newspaper tributes recording his service to city and state.

Then to Cedar Hill, Tennessee, one day came a letter from New Orleans. It was from a niece of the childless "Mr. Thompson"—she had always called him that, even when he courted her at Sewanee. It enclosed a sealed, stamped envelope the niece had found addressed to her, but unmailed. It had slipped into the rear slot of Thompson's heavy rolltop desk. The niece had retrieved it on dismantling his office. Miss Queenie did not have to open the letter to know what it said. He was properly sympathetic to hear of the death of her husband, he knew nothing of the thirty years of her married life, but he still loved her as much as when they parted. Would she write him and reassure him? Would it be acceptable for him to come to see her again? He waited in vain.

She auctioned her beautiful possessions, closed the great home at Washington Hall, and retired to a bedroom in her son's home, never to come out. When she died in 1959, I was a pallbearer on a bleak windy day in Nashville's Mount Olivet cemetery. After the grave was closed I had another duty to perform. The last time I had seen her in New Orleans she had given me about two dozen letters, each in its envelope and the packet tied with pink ribbon. They smelled of lavender. The frayed and time-stained paper spoke of many re-readings. "Arthur," she had said, "when I die I want you to burn these at Beckwith's Point." She didn't tell me not to read them. She knew I wouldn't.

ABC, Personal recollections.

The University has always been close to my heart. I have watched with pride the succeeding generations of students who have absorbed her traditions and that something called the Sewanee Spirit.

Queenie Woods Washington, in *Sewanee Cook Book.*

TOLERATION

ONE DAY Mrs. Woods was standing on her front porch. Looking down the street she saw her young son walking toward the house with General Grant holding his hand. She said to her daughters in dismay, "I'll bet Bobby brings the General into the house. What will the neighbors say!" Sure enough, the young man brought General Grant up on the porch and presented him. "Mother, I want you to meet my friend General Grant." Mrs. Woods was polite but didn't invite Grant in. Grant too was very polite and turned to leave after an exchange of pleasantries. He offered his hand to the eldest daughter and said, "I'd like to shake hands with Miss Georgia, Mrs. Woods, since she is the only one of your daughters who hasn't spit at me."

Queenie Woods Washington to ABC, January 27, 1952.

GIRLS AND DOLLS

MISS QUEENIE's mother and her older brothers and sisters (Queenie was the youngest of 9) lived right across the street from Union headquarters in Nashville during The War. Once the Woods sisters put two of their dolls on their front window sill with signs on them lettered "Old Man Lincoln" and "Mrs. Lincoln." The dolls fell by accident, as some soldiers were passing, and the men carried them to headquarters. The girls pled with their mother to retrieve the dolls. Mrs. Woods said indeed she would not, that the girls had no business insulting the president. Finally the children, gathering up their courage, went to headquarters and saw Grant himself. He gave the dolls back but said, "If ever again you do anything insulting to the president, you will hear from me, and very severely."

Queenie Woods Washington to ABC, January 26, 1952.

160

HOOKED

QUEENIE WOODS ought to have been a train dispatcher. She is said to have worn a half dozen fraternity pins at one time, always with the right one showing. One evening at Powhatan, she was receiving in the living room a swain who thought he was Number One. There appeared another who thought *he* was first in her affection, and he was brusque with the "interloper." By comparing notes they discovered their true position and turned on the young lady. She was about to salvage a difficult situation, when a third lad entered who also considered himself the sole claimant of her true affection. He took exception to the first two but soon was persuaded to make common cause. When all three confronted Miss Queenie, she fled in tears. General Kirby-Smith walked in as she retreated and was indignant at the students for bringing a lady to tears. "Why, General," said one of them. "Has she got you too?"

David A. Shepherd '00 to ABC, November 16, 1951. *Miss Queenie is said to have been the only woman ever initiated into Delta Tau Delta Fraternity. Unquestionably the ceremony was extra-legal, but there were no expulsions because of it.*

LIAISON

SEWANEE'S TELEGRAPH office, closed about 1955, had its ups and downs. In one of its troughs, a telegram clicked in over the key to Senor William W. Lewis from Queenie Woods Washington in Nashville. The sender, declining an invitation to a Delta Tau Delta function, had said "Tied up with Garden Club." The message, libelously altered, read "Tied up with Gordon Clark." ['27]

Queenie Woods Washington to ABC, February 20, 1952.

MOURNING

For women to "go into mourning" had become such a cherished Southern tradition by the late 19th century that it was not limited to widows. When Miss Queenie was twelve, her nine-year-old brother died in a sleighing accident. She went into mourning for two years. Then her father died and back she went into black until she was nineteen. She then got married and went abroad, coming back with "new clothes" for the first time.

Queenie Woods Washington to ABC, November 2, 1951.

LONG SEPARATION

Mrs. John B. Elliott, wife of the University's first health officer, was a Huger (pronounced You-Gee) from Charleston. She was one of twelve children whose parents lived on opposite ends of an island and did not speak to each other for twenty years. When Mr. Huger died, his long-separated widow still dutifully followed the rigid Southern custom of going into mourning, wearing black "down to her heels," and made no social calls all summer.

Queenie Woods Washington to ABC. Spring, 1952.

VULGARITY

We add to our vocabularies in different ways. Miss Queenie Woods was wading one day, at the mature age of 13, in a branch near Happy Hollow at Sewanee. Little Phoebe Elliott, 14, saw her and said, "Don't you know wading is VULGAR?" And so that word was added to the vocabulary of Miss Queenie.

Queenie Woods Washington to ABC, May 17, 1954.

CHANGE OF NAME

CHANGING ANYTHING at Sewanee is difficult, but changing a name is next to impossible. By the middle of the 1950's, I as director of public relations had grown tired of explaining why Sewanee Inn was a dormitory and Tuckaway across the street was an Inn. Furthermore, there was a strong hope that some generous benefactor would make possible a university motel, and if that should ever come about, the logical name should be available. I made up a list of about a dozen trustees and regents who were or had been in love with Miss Queenie. She was bedridden, she was a great letter-writer, and she thought that Bishop Stephen Elliott was the most neglected of the University's founders. She started writing. In the incredibly short space of a year the board had acted, stonemasons were at work carving Elliott Hall on Sewanee Inn, the Robert Woodward Barnwell Elliotts across the street were delighted, and there was now a logical place to hang Dr. Edward McCrady's oil portrait of the Bishop.

ABC, assorted notes and recollections.

MORALS AND DOGMA

FANNIE M. PRESTON, matron of St. Luke's Hall, obeyed implicitly the injunction that Sewanee adults would not drink with students. This did not alleviate her annual yearning for a bit of eggnog. Regularly on Christmas David A. Shepherd, who concocted the best, would pass beneath her window whistling "Onward Christian Soldiers." As he walked with an innocent looking paper bag through the students invariably assembled for tea in her living room, she would rise, accompany him to the kitchen, whisk the delicacy into her icebox and, after the students left, would regale herself with Mr. Shepherd's famous specialty.

David A. Shepherd '00 to ABC, June 3, 1952.

DISLOCATED

GENERAL WILLIAM T. SHERMAN headed a Louisiana military academy before the Civil War, and Mary Gayle Aiken knew him then. During the war the Aiken plantation in South Carolina was in the line of march. General Sherman himself came to the house, but Mrs. Aiken would not let him in. He stood outside to talk. She asked why he made war on women and children. He spared the house but took all chickens, livestock, and food. A few days later stragglers came through and burned the house. After the war the land was confiscated for taxes, and Mrs. Aiken, the sister of Mrs. Josiah Gorgas, went to Sewanee with her two children, Gayle and Carrie. With Mrs. Fannie Preston she kept Tremlett Hall until she went to New Orleans to live.

Queenie Woods Washington to ABC, November 14, 1951.

ANXIOUS

Two of the McCrady girls—Posie and Sabina—set off for Charleston to visit their grandfather McCrady for two months—travelling with Miss Connie Miles. The whole family went to the Cowan Depot to see them off.

I found to my astonishment and vexation, that the Agent at Cowan had no through tickets to Charleston and not even a single ticket to Atlanta. . . . It is thus that that RR Co. permits its employees to mismanage one of the most promising and valuable travellers stations in the whole State. So I was obliged to buy tickets to Chattanooga, and give them to the girls, requesting the conductor to see them provided at Chattanooga with tickets. They went off leaving me feeling very anxious. There were no ladies on the train but themselves; and I cannot tell what may happen to three inexperienced girls on so long a journey —but they are in God's hands.

John McCrady Diary, October 16, 1878.

164

BEARERS OF TIDINGS

M ISS KATHLEEN MCCRADY lived the better part of an eon in the old frame house built by her mother on the site of the present McCrady Hall. Her temper was not always temperate, and indeed there were those who would hesitate before accosting her. Such a one was John Sutherland of the University Press who was observed one day standing in front of her house watching smoke billowing out of several windows and from the roof. Mary Gibson Kirby Koski joined him and after a discreet interval asked if he intended to tell Miss Kathleen that her house was on fire. Mr. Sutherland, doubtless recalling what happened to messengers of old who brought bad tidings, said indeed he was not. Mary Gibson, volunteering to go along, accompanied him to the front door. She called, "Miss Kathleen?" There was no reply. Louder, with knocking. Finally from far upstairs, "What do you want?"

"We came to tell you that your house is on fire," said Mrs. Koski.

With unexpected sweetness Miss McCrady inquired, "Oh, is it on fire down there too?"

Marymor Sanborn Cravens to ABC, February 22, 1972.

BLACKMAIL

M ISS SADA ELLIOTT was upbraiding her niece Charlee Shoup for having taken an unchaperoned walk with a student. Unfortunately there stood in the back yard of the Elliott place a log cabin, used by Miss Sada for her writing, to which occasionally she repaired, presumably to show a manuscript to one of her numerous suitors. Miss Charlee was not above blackmail. Shaking her finger under the nose of her redoubtable aunt, she said, "Sada Elliott, if you tell one word about me, I'll tell what I saw through the chink of the cabin." From that day onward, Miss Sada was the soul of toleration toward Charlee.

Queenie Woods Washington to ABC, December 16, 1951. *This writer has not been able to confirm or deny the legend that Point Disappointment overlooking Lost Cove received its name from Miss Sada's rejection of a suitor there.*

THEY MAKETH MAN

ALTHOUGH STUDENT pranks received a measure of chiding, bad manners were a different matter. They were utterly forbidden, completely disapproved. Arrayed against lapses of etiquette were some two dozen determined ladies. No such course was listed in the catalog, nor did its professors wear cap and gown, but manners were emphatically taught at Sewanee. All the students ate in private homes where various stratagems were employed to let the young barbarians know how young gentlemen should act. "Aunt Mattie" (Mrs. McNeely DuBose) regularly and by arrangement, corrected her two sons, Mac and Theodore, for any *faux pas* committed by her boarders. Miss Maria Porcher made the boys with the worst manners sit next to her where they could observe her usage and be gently corrected.

Young Percival Elliott Huger '03 should have known better. No word was ever spoken to him, but he knew, as did everyone else including his embarrassed family back on their Savannah rice plantation, why he wasn't invited to the party. Mrs. Telfair Hodgson, despite her widowhood, kept the most elegant home at Sewanee. She invited every student to a meal during his first year. If he made his party call, he was invited again. When sprightly young Emma Huger came to visit her freshman brother Percy, Mrs. Hodgson gave her a great reception. Although just the resident kin of the Elliotts and Hugers would have made a crowd, *everyone* was invited, everyone, that is, except brother Percy. It is to be surmised that every student in the college and grammar school, and particularly the members of the A.T.O. fraternity, who didn't know what a party call was, found out.

May Peronneau DuBose to ABC, May 20, 1955. David A. Shepherd to ABC, about 1950.

INCREDULITY

WILL PERCY '04 went from Sewanee to Harvard and came back for a visit, staying at Powhatan with Mrs. Hale. She asked him, "Will, you didn't *really* meet any gentlemen there, did you?"

Maryon Moise to ABC, May 20, 1957.

JUMPERS

C<small>ARRIE AND</small> J<small>OSEPHINE</small> K<small>IRBY</small>-S<small>MITH</small> would rarely walk through the gate in front of their house, preferring to step or jump across the fence, swinging their legs and long skirts over the top rail.

George A. Wilson '03 to ABC, April 2, 1960.

MAKE MUCH OF TIME

C<small>ARRIE</small> K<small>IRBY</small>-S<small>MITH</small>, after a rather long engagement, was to marry William Crolly, the chapel organist. She invited a few guests, but the day *before* the wedding, she announced, "I am going to be married today." She called the chaplain to come to the Oratory and sent word for Mr. Crolly to meet her at Powhatan. A steady drizzle was coming down, but they started across the park without an umbrella, she about ten feet ahead of him. The invited guests felt tricked but never knew why she did it. I know. It was because she liked to appear eccentric, but fundamentally she was not. She was unselfish and loving.

Queenie Woods Washington to ABC, November 14, 1951.

SWEET NINA

R<small>ANDOLPH</small> B<small>UCK</small> '91 was in General Kirby-Smith's math class. They did not like each other. Nina, the General's daughter, was engaged to an Atlanta man. One day Randolph got up, went to the stove, threw his textbook in the fire, and walked out of class. He went to the General's house, hitched the General's horse to "the hearse" as the carriage was called, drove with Nina to Winchester and married her. All was pre-arranged. They were not forgiven until Nina returned a couple of years later, bringing a darling baby daughter, the first grandchild. Mrs. Kirby-Smith said, "Nina, you are eating your white bread now." Nina and Randolph returned to Mississippi, had reverses, and Nina wrote: "Mother, that white bread is getting grayer and grayer."

Queenie Woods Washington to ABC, November 14, 1951.

CLARA'S POINT

No ONE who knew him would have called Bishop Quintard a despotic character. He was not however a man to put himself in the path of onrushing fate. When it began to appear that young professor Benjamin Lawton Wiggins was (a) showing administrative talent and (b) spending some time with daughter Clara, he was not above making a minor arrangement or two.

Among Sewanee historians there are two schools of thought on the manner in which Mr. Wiggins proposed. Their diversity is good illustration of the dilemma which awaits the careful scholar at every turn of history. According to one of these, Clara Quintard and Lawton, as he was called by those who did not use the less formal Billy Wiggs, habitually walked in the afternoons past Morgan's Steep to a rocky promontory now known as Clara's Point. There, on a Sunday, the timid and procrastinating male finally put the question. Somewhat to his surprise, he received no oral answer but was led to the edge of the rock, where in easy reach, was carved the eloquent and immemorial "YES."

According to the other school, the proposal took place in this wise. Mr. Wiggins had been "seeing" Miss Clara. Both schools agree on this much. One evening they were in amiable discussion in the Bishop's living room at Fulford Hall when the prelate himself walked in upon them, as may have been the custom in those days, and, as man to man, asked Mr. Wiggins what his intentions were. Wiggins, fourteen years younger than Clara, was doubtless wondering himself what they were when Clara nodded and plans for the marriage were under way.

These may seem to be trivialities, but it was not long before Bishop Quintard became the first Bishop of the deep South to request a Coadjutor. Everyone knew that the outstanding candidate would be the young Vice-Chancellor of the University of the South, Rev. Thomas Frank Gailor. In due course, Dr. Gailor's election vacated the Vice-Chancellorship and there, figuratively standing at the door of the outer office, was Bishop Quintard's son-in-law.

From assorted notes, none reliable.

168

Y.E.S.

R AINSFORD FAIRBANKS GLASS DUDNEY, who won't let a good story be, has this to say apropos of the beautiful account of the "YES" at Clara's Point. "That word on the rock was not acceptance of B. L. Wiggins' proposal at all. It simply stood for the first names of three friends who loved to walk out there. They were Ydie Maria Randolph (pronounced Eedie), Eva Fairbanks, and Sam Swann."

Mrs. R. G. Dudney to ABC, June 29, 1962.

SEWANEE SEGREGATION

R ACE AND CLASS relations at Sewanee have not very often run counter to common Southern experience, but good will and ingenuity have been recorded. When Miss Lily Green was at Kendal, a problem came to her attention which she handled with some adroitness. A workman on the Mountain was of Indian descent, and his skin was dark. When his small children were of school age and applied for entrance to the local school, they were denied. On hearing this, Miss Lily took the children under her wing and instructed them in the 3 R's in a private class. Segregation was unshaken, of course, but its tragedy was mitigated.

Miss Fanny deRosset to ABC, undated note.

NON DISPUTANDUM EST

T HE WAY of the historiographer is not always easy. On May 14, 1952, Queenie Woods Washington told me: "Mrs. George R. Fairbanks' daughter Anna (by her first marriage) was wed to Leonidas Cotten ('73) in the Sewanee cemetery." A beautiful story. Consultation with the living authority on Fairbanks-Beard-Wright connections brought this un-verification.

"Arthur, I wish this rumor could be squelched. There is NO truth

169

in it. Anna Beard Wright, daughter of Susan Beard Wright and the Rev. Benjamin Wright (Mrs. Fairbanks' first husband) was married to Leonidas Cotten, son of the Mrs. Cotten who kept students. I tried to find out if the marriage of Anna Wright and Leonidas was recorded in Grundy or Franklin County. It was not. It was evidently a run-away marriage but I am quite sure it was NOT in the Sewanee cemetery." (Signed) Rainsford Glass Dudney.

More's the pity.

LALLIE

M ISS SALLY MILHADO, called "Lallie Miladdie" by the three nieces she reared—Ena, Mary, and Etta—was unique. Archie Butt '86 said that she didn't need to read a book. She *was* one. Cary Grayson '03, who had boarded at her hall (later the senior DuVal Cravens home), arranged for her to meet President Wilson in Washington, cautioning her to be dignified, and doubtless also warning him what to expect. When ushered in, she clapped him on the back and said, "I'm glad to see you, old top."

At Sewanee she was very fond of the Kirby-Smiths, especially Rennie and his sister Fanny. When Fanny announced her forthcoming marriage, Miss Sally was furious and went to the Catholic monastery in Winchester so that she could not be reached to be invited to the wedding. She thought she should have been consulted prior to the announcement.

Queenie Woods Washington to ABC, October 10, 1957.

SANCTIFIED

W HILE MISS SALLY was in Washington for her visit to see the President, she stayed with Admiral and Mrs. Cary T. Grayson across from the Swiggetts on T Street. She went for a ride in the President's car, and when she actually shook hands with Wilson she was wearing a new pair of kid gloves bought for the occasion. She took off the gloves, never wearing them again, taking great pride in showing them to her friends.

Dr. Glen L. Swiggett to ABC, October 10, 1957.

SCOREBOARD

Miss Sally Milhado had other remarkable traits beside her enthusiasm for Louisiana cigarettes in a day when smoking was not quite the thing for ladies. She was an exuberant football enthusiast. When the famous team of 1899 returned in triumph she was among students and residents who gathered around a huge bonfire in front of the Supply Store. She wore an old cap on her dishevelled hair and joined in singing, dancing, and cheering. Someone came along with an old white mule and, with Miss Josephine Kirby-Smith, she painted the scores of the games on the sides and flanks with black paint which he carried about the campus for many days.

Rev. J. N. Atkins '02 to ABC, December 8, 1956.

NEVER UNDERESTIMATE

At Sewanee the minority is always right. Miss Johnnie Tucker, who while matron was known as the Empress of Tuckaway, was forced into retirement at the prime of life, about seventy, by blindness. Her little white cottage behind the dormitory became a Mecca for returning alumni. At one magic moment, to relieve overcrowding on library walls, the oil portrait of a Sewanee bishop was hung over the fireplace of her dormitory. From Miss Johnnie's cottage, with its mementoes of Sewanee's past, came the imperious command, "Take that portrait down!" It came down. No one knew, or asked, why. Miss Johnnie is also alleged to have expelled one hapless student by the simple expedient of packing his trunk and having it moved to the yard.

ABC from undated notes, about 1948.

REJECTED

M EDORA HODGSON was a lady like no other. Always the natural belle of any ball, she combined beauty, wit, and astuteness. When the *Centennial Alumni Directory* was delivered to her, she spent a couple of days meticulously searching the pages. Finally she had to confess. "Every man who ever proposed to me is now dead." Recalling the names of some, we inquired about a particularly distinguished alumnus who was of their number. "Why did you turn him down, Miss Medora?" Instantly she replied, "Because he wore striped socks."

Medora Cheatham Hodgson to ABC, Fall, 1958.

GAMBLING

B OTH MISS MEDORA CHEATHAM and Professor William Boone Nauts had reputations for loquacity. A student, Bobby McMillan, and his summer girl, Bessie Lindsley, made a friendly wager at a Sewanee dance on which of their two young friends could beat the other at holding the conversation. Miss Medora was warned of the wager, but Professor Nauts was not. Now Nauts could talk well and long on any subject, but when it came to baseball his accomplishment was prodigious. During intermission, the two were brought together and walked off with the gambler couple behind them. Miss Cheatham was in rare form and for upwards of a half hour was heard to deliver an unbroken evaluation of social life in Nashville. As she paused for breath, her hitherto silent partner said of the last person mentioned, "Oh, I've met her." For once, Miss Medora let her guard down. "Where?" she asked. "At the baseball game," said Nauts. Bessie turned to the beaming Bobby and said, "Here's your money."

David A. Shepherd '00 to ABC, November 18, 1951.

172

BENEFIT

M ISS QUEENIE says that Sewanee lost the better part of $2,500 through the inequity of Jupiter Pluvius. It happened this way. Miss Charlotte Gailor agreed to put on a "Benefit" for the University, a mediaeval pageant in Nashville on the lawn of the fashionable Belle Meade Country Club. Mrs. Governor Benton McMillin, quite a beauty, refused to wear glasses to read her part, literally hundreds of lines. To save her pride, she memorized the lines, and the show went on. The performance was insured for $2,500 against rain. On that Sunday afternoon, there was a two-inch downpour in Nashville. Most would-be guests, presuming the rain was general, stayed away, but the insurance was not collectible. Not a drop fell inside the property lines of the Belle Meade Country Club.

Queenie Woods Washington to ABC, February 11, 1953.

MONEY AND BANKING

C HARLIE HILL from the valley delivered produce to Sewanee homes. Charlotte Gailor was a regular customer. Once, paying by check, she inadvertently *signed* it "Charlie Hill." The bank cashed it and debited her account. When she caught the discrepancy a month later, she telephoned the cashier. He said, "We knew it was all right. We recognized your handwriting and didn't want to bother you with a phone call."

Charlotte Gailor to ABC, August 1, 1956.

PENALTIES OF PRIVILEGE

N ANNIE GAILOR, the bishop's oldest daughter, tripped on a stair-rug and muttered, "Hell." Her father said, "Nannie, remember that you are a bishop's daughter." She replied, "If I had forgotten that, I would have said worse than Hell."

Dr. Robert W. Daniel '35 to ABC, August 12, 1972.

173

RAIN

A BOUT 1886, Madame Frances Sylva (D'Arusmont) Guthrie, arrived on the Mountain with her two sons Kenneth and William Norman. The old train which brought the trio up the Mountain unloaded them in a blinding rain storm. They trudged up the hill from the station and the first house bearing any semblance of life was the Pillet home. The three splashed up the box-hedged path and rapped at the door. The popular tailor, seeing strangers, turned to his wife and in French asked what he should do about taking them in, adding "one would not turn a dog out on such a night." The Baroness, who had been born in Paris, answered him in impeccable French and the hospitality of the home was theirs.

Mary Marrs to Fanny deRosset, July 19, 1954.

BUSTLE OF THE BARONESS

M RS. WILLIAM EUGENE GUTHRIE, *née* Frances Sylva D'Arusmont, was the daughter of the famous Fannie Wright of Nashoba, pioneer of the woman's liberation movement. In 1889 she built the house which came to be called the Colmore House and which burned in December 1971. She lived in it only briefly with her two brilliant sons (William Norman and Kenneth Sylvan) and then sold it to the widowed Mrs. Robert Woodward Barnwell Elliott. Baroness D'Arusmont, as she liked to be called, developed back pains at the age of fifty-five and was loaned a hot water bottle by Mrs. Telfair Hodgson, her neighbor. Invited to a party at Chaplain Gailor's, she ingeniously substituted the bag for her bustle. Pain was alleviated uutil the rubber bottle broke, attracting a good bit of attention.

Queenie Woods Washington to ABC, probably in 1952.

THE PANES LINGER ON

T HE "FRANK LLOYD WRIGHT house at Sewanee" continues to startle people viewing a display of the famous architect's plans at this museum or that. The house was designed for Baroness D'Arusmont's son, the Rev. William Norman Guthrie, who was on the faculty (1908-1911). I first saw the drawings in the Metropolitan Museum of Art in New York and had them copied for the Sewanee Archives. The same plans were finally used for a famous showplace in Oak Park, Illinois. In the Sollace Freeman house which stands at the south end of Hardee Field near where the Guthrie place was to have been built, there once were diamond-shaped window panes just like those in the Illinois house.

ABC, miscellaneous notes.

PRIORITIES

THE WARE house was always filled with relatives. When Mary was about to be born, the family was vacationing at Flat Rock, N. C., and on hand were house guests galore—mother-in-law, grandmother "Madame Ware," Aunt Lettie, and Uncle John. The day finally came. Doctor and nurse arrived. The nurse went upstairs for the vigil while the doctor joined the relatives in a card game downstairs. In due course, the nurse came down the steps to announce, "The baby is coming," and motioned for the doctor to hurry. Madame Ware objected: "He can't go yet. Wait until he's dummy."

Mary Ware Daniel to ABC, August 15, 1972.

NOT YET

ALTHOUGH SEWANEE is thought by many to be the last way station on the highroad to heaven, Mountain residents have never been noted for their desire to leave this world for the happier one beyond. Miss Sarah Nicholls was paying a sad visit to grandmother Cheatham, ninety-odd, who had just lost her daughter, a lady in her seventies.

"Don't grieve, Mrs. Cheatham," Miss Nicholls said consolingly, "It won't be for long."

Sitting bolt upright with indignation, Mrs. Cheatham said, "Just a moment, young lady. I don't want to die."

David A. Shepherd '00 to ABC, November 18, 1951.

175

IF DEBATABLE— NO!

SOME WARS were over by 1930 but not THE war. The Music Group at Sewanee debated the wisdom of instituting variety in its annual program. Why not, someone asked, substitute "The Battle Hymn of the Republic" for "America." The fear of a slugfest with Mrs. Crolly or Mrs. Hale at Powhatan, daughters of General Kirby-Smith, prompted a negative decision. The observation of David Shepherd was, "Like a proposal of marriage, if the question can be debated, the answer is *No*."

David A. Shepherd '00 to ABC, November 1, 1953.

FUNERAL FOR THE UDC

PEOPLE WHO die at Sewanee are customarily considerate. For instance, there was Mrs. Jack Eggleston. She was the widow of Confederate Navy Captain Jack Eggleston, the last surviving officer of high rank of the Confederate Navy and skipper of the *Merrimac*. Mrs. Eggleston, about 95, was honorary president of the UDC. When she was unable to go to the convention, it came to her. After elaborate preparations, the United Daughters converged on Sewanee for their annual meeting. Mrs. Eggleston died on the first day, to provide one of Sewanee's greatest funerals. Mrs. Joseph Eggleston, niece-in-law of the deceased, was appointed to furnish the standees for the all-night vigil at the casket. She, as matron of Magnolia Dining Hall, selected the necessary number of students, few of whom knew the aged lady. The day of the funeral, all the students who had stood vigil the night before were gratifyingly attentive. "Mrs. E." had arranged on the night the body lay in state to send to the chapel the most magnificent assortment of viands imaginable. For the students, the affair had taken on the atmosphere of a banquet.

Charles Edward Thomas '27 to ABC, August 2, 1953.

CLARA

S HE WAS born in the valley within sight of Green's View. It might have been about 1915, for certainly she was a mature and poised lady by the late 1930's, when she was "discovered" by Sewanee students. She presided with infinite grace over a small restaurant at the side of the road below Monteagle on the Nashville slope. It was a rustic little place with rafters from which a student could hang by his knees until she frowned. Generations of young gentlemen loved her to the point of veneration. After 1940, very few returned to the campus without stopping to see Clara. Her husband, Tom, was as sturdy and rough-hewn as she was delicate and demure. She prospered and in due course bought the big mansion on the Monteagle Highway across from the DuBose Conference Center. It was said to have been the stopover of gangster Al Capone, when he drove between Chicago and Miami. She named it Claramont. Her circle of admirers soon expanded to include the bishops and clergy of Tennessee. She catered meals and banquets for the laymen and the churchwomen until Ernie and Winnie Walker came to manage the Conference Center.

Among her most devoted admirers were Bishop and Mrs. Frank A. Juhan. It was he who determined that she should be translated six miles to the Domain of the University of the South. With money mysteriously supplied from unknown benefactors, the beautiful Sewanee Inn and Claramont Restaurant materialized at the edge of Preston Mooney's golf course. Its first customers were the House of Bishops, meeting in the Centennial of 1957. Sewanee Inn was such a roaring success that soon the old Warriner place, overlooking Lost Cove, was acquired, remodeled, and landscaped. It became The Castle, and for its elegance was known through the mid-South. Not all good things come to an end, but the reign of the lovely Clara finally did. Tom died. The good Bishop died. Clara moved away to Atlanta, remarried and moved to California. She had become a legend in her lifetime.

ABC, assorted notes and many memories of Clara Shoemate.

CAULDRON BUBBLE

M RS. VAN NESS, mother of Mrs. Rogers, was called by students the Witch of Endor. She was quite a recluse but once in a while she came out and walked down the street with her feet wrapped in tow sacks to keep warm and carrying a Sewanee lantern, a staff, and wearing a long black veil. On a foggy night she resembled a scene from *Macbeth*.

Chaplain E. M. Bearden '15 to ABC, January 20, 1961.

COLOR LINE

A BOUT 1948 a nation-wide fad of buying gaudily colored chicks for children at Easter penetrated the University Supply Store. Of course, the buyer should have remembered that Miss Annie Underwood was sensitive about cruelty to animals. She made her visitation the very day of their arrival and said, "Send those birds back where they came from!" The entrepreneur lost no time complying with her demand. "If those chicks are going to be squeezed to death by children, it won't be in Sewanee," she vowed.

ABC, from undated notes.

NO NUDES

M RS. EMMA HOLLAND, who lived with Miss Louise Finley, was a modest lady. On one occasion the Woman's Club was having an open meeting to which men had been invited. Mrs. Holland arrived to find that the subject was to be Renoir, and a number of the artist's famous nudes were on display. At furious pace she went around the room, turning the more offensive paintings to the wall. The ladies let her get away with it, and the gentlemen pretended that backsides of paintings were to be expected.

Louise S. McDonald to ABC, December 15, 1946.

ON TOAST

People have different talents. Some are artists, some musicians, some athletes. Charlotte Patten Guerry's talent was that of hospitality. Her instincts were nearly infallible, and her memory for detail prodigious. I came through Sewanee in 1943 on Navy leave and again in 1944. Both times I was invited to stay with the Guerrys at Fulford Hall. The first time Mrs. Guerry asked me what I wanted for breakfast—hot tea, cereal, and two poached eggs on toast. The second time a year later, she didn't ask. I was served hot tea, cereal, and two poached eggs on toast.

ABC, grateful recollections.

CHARLOTTE PATTEN GUERRY

For some highly creative people sculpture is an outlet, or music, or writing. For Mrs. Alexander Guerry it was the stimulating of productive human relationships. Aided by a phenomenal memory, a driving will, enormous energy and an encompassing sense of responsibility to her husband and his work, she arranged with exquisite taste a continuing flow of contacts among people which placed the stamp of her special genius on nearly everything that happened at Sewanee for ten years.

She set a personal example of humanity and concern. Let a University secretary be hospitalized and chances were about even that her first visitor would be Mrs. Guerry. Let a child be sick and Mrs. Guerry came by to see what was needed. She carried on a prodigious correspondence by hand, and communicated by nearly every means—by personal visit, telephone, telegraph, notes, gifts and flowers.

It would be difficult to count the number of young alumni who brought their brides to see her on their honeymoon. Unless a visitor to the Mountain was otherwise cared for, she considered everyone her personal responsibility. Tuckaway Inn constituted then the community's only public housing facility. She was able to convert that

179

handicap into a memorable advantage with her genius for propriety combined with a thoughtfulness and concern for the individual. For her, hospitality—particularly in her home—was a way of life.

At Commencement time Mrs. Guerry was indefatigable. She knew well in advance who was coming, and with or without wife. She knew where everyone was staying. A trustee would find himself seated next to the widow of his classmate. The new math instructor (if his wife were entertaining a trustee couple) would meet in her home a distinguished engineer or architect.

Most of her seated dinners for ten to sixty people were planned to such perfection that the buzz level was unbelievable. Perfect strangers, finding themselves seated next to each other, found in a matter of minutes that they had more in common with each other than they had with some of their best friends. Her grasp of and her mnemonic recording of the complexities of human personality were rare talents and an incredible boon to Sewanee.

ABC. *Sewanee News, May 1970. Mrs. Guerry is one of five women identifiable in the Historical Windows in the Narthex of All Saints' Chapel. The others are Charlotte Morris Manigault, Olivia Procter Benedict, Frances Potter Hodgson, and Jessie Ball duPont.*

HOW DO I LOVE THEE

SUSAN RAINSFORD FAIRBANKS, daughter of the famous Florida historian who was a founder of the University of the South, died after the birth of her first child, and shortly thereafter the baby died too. Her husband, Charles Minnegerode Beckwith, headmaster of the Grammar School and later Bishop of Alabama (1902-22), was understandably inconsolable. He took her wedding silver, had it melted down and made into a chalice and paten, and caused to be set in the stem of the chalice her engagement diamond and her wedding ring. It is still the most used chalice at services of the Holy Communion in All Saints' Chapel.

Rainsford Fairbanks Glass Dudney to ABC, confirmed in summer 1978.

AFTERWORD

As EARLY as 1950 I realized that a book on the lighter side of Sewanee history was in order. Reprinting *Purple Sewanee*, then twenty years old, and *The Sewanee Cook Book*, ten years older, brought old lore to new generations. There still has accumulated, especially in letters and in oral stories, a kind of anecdotal material which deserves transmission to posterity but which has little place in formal history.

Stories like the ride of the Shapard children down the Mountain on a wild hand car and of Miss Mucidore's visit to the Sewanee hospital illumine much about the times and the environs which cannot be shown by other means.

I had hardly settled at the desk of the Alumni Secretary in 1946 when I began collecting stories. The oldest living alumnus then was John S. Bradford, matriculant No. 33, of Springfield, Illinois, who had witnessed President Lincoln's funeral. I urged him to search his memory and tell me what he found. His letters were so fresh and pleasant that I systematically asked other alumni to unburden themselves.

Into the alumni file folders went every scrap of information that could be turned up. When a letter came containing human interest or historical data, I dictated an appropriate note for my personal collection, which by 1965 contained 15,000 pieces. The bulging files almost crowded us out of Elliott Hall.

The accumulation of data necessary for the *Centennial Alumni Directory*, edited by my wife and Helen Petry, added impetus to the collection of anecdotes. Thousands of letters were solicited from widows, children, and grandchildren of early alumni, professors, and trustees. Throughout this period Sarah Hodgson Torian, whose grandfather Potter had made a pre-Civil War pledge to the University, was also collecting. She as volunteer Archivist had established a locked cage in the basement of the old library in 1940. The Torians and the Chittys, back and forth across South Carolina Avenue, excitedly compared acquisitions for nearly fifteen years.

There was no Southern diocese in which we did not have a history buff ready to look up a record for us or find the married name and address of some person we were seeking. Sewanee attics were loaded with letters, diaries, and scrapbooks. There must have been fifty people living at Sewanee in 1950 who had direct connections with Sewanee prior to 1880. Circumstances were ideal for gathering memorabilia. My secretary, Miss Fanny deRosset, had an uncanny faculty for locating the Lost.

I doubt if there are a dozen institutions of higher learning in America whose history is as well documented as Sewanee's. For instance, the Minutes of almost every Trustees' meeting from the beginning are in print. The Episcopalian peculiarity of requiring every diocese to publish a Journal in turn almost demands that every bishop keep a diary. When to such rich lodes of source material are added such treasures as the John McCrady Diary, a half dozen student diaries, and the fabulous, million-word document of Bishop Charles Todd Quintard, the anecdote collector has a field day. Some of the selections which have appeared elsewhere in print are here excerpted and may be found in fuller form in the publications cited.

Selecting items for a book like this involved setting up criteria. Here are those I used. (1) How interesting or amusing is the story? (2) Has it been published? Preference is given to material either unpublished or relatively inaccessible, such as old *Proceedings* or diocesan *Journals*. (3) Does the subject or source have special significance? If Dr. Rennie Kirby-Smith said it or Professor John McCrady wrote it, I consider it "special" because of their importance on the Sewanee scene of their respective times. (4) Does it explode a myth or lay a rumor? Much as I hated to destroy the Morgan's Steep legend, it had to be done. From present evidence, I can't believe that General Morgan rode his horse off that cliff. (5) Whether historical fact or amusing fiction, is it true to the spirit of the place? If not, out it went.

The pattern of chapter headings developed both chronologically and by subject. "Early Times" is confined to what happened before The War. "Environs" begins after that episode but is expanded to include the People as well as the Place. Atmosphere is not separable because both the physical place and the persons inhabiting it were contributing factors. The chapter on "Professors" includes some whose teaching was at the Hospital. "Students" obviously include former students—alumni. Into "Bishops" we have dropped a few non-Episcopal trustees

182

who kept them on an even keel. Naturally "Ladies" are all women who have loved Sewanee.

The obligation which this book owes to the keen memories and discerning observations of Queenie Woods Washington, R. M. Kirby-Smith '95, O. N. Torian '96, and especially my predecessor as Organizing Secretary of the Associated Alumni, David A. Shepherd '00, is apparent if one consults the index. "Uncle David" encouraged me to record the stories of an earlier Sewanee long before I found myself at Tulane University seeking a subject for a master's thesis. *Reconstruction at Sewanee: The Founding of the University of the South and its First Administration 1857-72* was the first of a projected series of scholarly treatment of Sewanee history. This book is intended to supplement the classics in Sewaneeana: George R. Fairbanks' *History of the University of the South; Purple Sewanee,* edited by Charlotte Gailor and others in 1932; Moultrie Guerry's *Men Who Made Sewanee;* and Waring McCrady's *Under the Sun at Sewanee.*

Nearly everything used here can be verified or supplemented in the University Archives. Stories which I heard, I tried to write down while they were fresh, but there always are chances for error. I will welcome corrections and additions in the hope that there will be reprintings for audiences fit though few.

December 30, 1977   ARTHUR BEN CHITTY
Fulford Cottage
Sewanee, Tennessee 37375

INDEX

Members of families cited on the same pages are grouped together.

Crow Creek, 47; Crow Creek Valley, 45
Crownover, Arthur, 84, 131
Cuba, Missionary District of, 128
Cumberland Forest Festival, 149
Cumberland Mountain, 8; Mountains, 19; Plateau, 1, 9; River, 1
Cumberland University, 91, 95
Curlyque Road, 48
Curtis, Moses Ashley, 6
Custer, H. L., 8

Dabney, Robert, 29, 30
Dabney, Thomas Ewing, 84
Dakin, Walter Edwin, 115
Dandridge, Edmund Pendleton, 132
Daniel, Mary Dabney Ware (Mrs. R. W.), 66, 175
Daniel, Nannie Cunningham (Mrs. R. W.), 173
Daniel, Robert Woodham, 36, 42, 126, 173
Davis, Ione Finley (Mrs. Roy Benton); Roy Benton, Jr., 126
Davis, Jeff, saloon, 63, 86
Davis, Jefferson, 21, 50, 119, 140, 141
Davis, Robert, 90
Davis, Thomas Frederick, 6
Decherd, Tenn., 9, 43
Decherd family, 9
Degrees, 107-108, 113, 130-131
Delaware Indians, 1, 2
Delta Tau Delta Fraternity, 161
DeMoville, Mary, 59
Depot, Sewanee, 10, 18, 85
deRosset, Fanny, 38, 102, 106, 169, 174, 182
deRosset, William Green, 85
Dickinson, Overton, 99
Divinity, Doctor of, 107
Dix, William Giles, 1
Dixie Highway, 65
Doggett, John Locke, 79
Dogs, 100-102
Domain, 15, 20, 22, 28, 65, 129
Douglas, Byrd, Scholarship, 144
Douglas, Charlotte Ferris, 155
Douglass, Charles Hervey, 105
Dowdell, Lavinia Shapard; William C., 11
DuBose, May Peronneau, 51, 166
DuBose, Mrs. McNeely; McNeely, 166
DuBose, Nannie Peronneau (Mrs. W. P.), 51
DuBose, William Haskell, 38, 51, 86
DuBose, Susie, 51
DuBose, Theodore Marion, 166
DuBose, William Porcher, 24, 49, 51, 52, 55, 56

DuBose Conference Center, Monteagle, 177
Dudney, Rainsford Fairbanks Glass (Mrs. Thomas Earl), 48, 108, 157, 169
Dueling, 56
Duncan, Herman C., 7
Dunn, Joseph Wood, 6
duPont, Jessie Ball (Mrs. Alfred Irenee), 146, 180; Library, 38, 149

E.Q.B. Club (Ecce Quam Bonum), 51, 57
Eastbrook, Tenn., 9
Eggleston, Mary Lewis Nunnally (Mrs. Robert Bolling), 176
Eggleston, Mrs. Jack, 176
Egleston, DuBose; William, 145
Electricity, 65
Elliott, Charlotte (Mrs. Charles McD. Puckette), 31
Elliott, Charlotte Bull Barnwell (Mrs. Stephen), 30, 31, 51
Elliott, Esther "Hesse" (Mrs. Francis A. Shoup), 30, 31
Elliott, John Barnwell, 31, 52, 56, 102, 108; Mrs. J. B., 31, 52
Elliott, Phoebe, 162
Elliott, Robert Habersham, 33, 102
Elliott, Robert Woodward Barnwell; Mrs. R. W. B., 29, 163
Elliott, Robert Woodward Barnwell (Bishop), 49; Mrs. R. W. B., 174
Elliott, Sarah Barnwell ("Sada"), 29-33, 36, 48, 165
Elliott, Stephen, 6, 11, 117, 136, 163
Elliott Hall, 65, 82, 89, 101, 163, 181
Elliott Park, 35
Emerald-Hodgson Hospital, 40, 43, 65, 136, 143, 150, 152
Emery Annex, 65
Endowment, 8
English, Stephanie, 127
Episcopal Church, services, 15, mission churches, 44, 103
Estill, Wallis, 4, 9
Estill Springs, Tenn., 9
Ezzell, John Moran, 105

Fairbanks, Charles Massey, 111
Fairbanks, Eva Lee (Mrs. James Gamewell Glass), 169
Fairbanks, Flora, 38
Fairbanks, George Rainsford, 5, 26, 32, 34, 53, 78, 107, 180, 183
Fairbanks, Susan Beard Wright (Mrs. G. R.), 169
Fairbanks, Susan Rainsford (Mrs. Charles Minnegerode Beckwith), 180

187

188

189

190

191

192

194

PATRONS

The Rt. Rev. and Mrs. John M. Allin, New York, New York

The Rev. C. FitzSimons and Martha Parker Allison, New York, New York

Mr. and Mrs. Robert M. Ayres, Jr., Sewanee

Mr. and Mrs. W. Alan Baird, Bryn Mawr, Pennsylvania

Mr. and Mrs. James C. Baird, Jr., Sewanee

Robert and Mary Ann Ballard, Goulds, Florida

The Rev. and Mrs. Robert F. Bartusch, Memphis, Tennessee

The Rev. and Mrs. Lee A. Belford, New York, New York

Mr. and Mrs. Samuel Benedict, Cincinnati, Ohio

Mr. Harold E. Bettle, Tenafly, New Jersey

The Rev. and Mrs. Charles H. Blakeslee, Jr., Evergreen, Colorado

Dr. and Mrs. John F. Blankenship, Phoenix, Arizona

Mr. Thomas Edward Britt, Windermere, Florida

The Rev. Mr. and Mrs. A. Stanley Bullock, Jr., Jacksonville, Florida

Mr. and Mrs. Frank Byerley, Lake Providence, Louisiana

Dr. Hugh H. Caldwell, Sewanee, Tennessee

The Rev. James G. Callaway, Jr., Oradell, New Jersey

Mr. and Mrs. G. Bowdoin Craighill, Jr., Washington, D. C.

Dr. and Mrs. Robert W. Daniel, Gambier, Ohio

Dr. and Mrs. Samuel M. Day, Jacksonville, Florida

Mrs. Jayne Moise Falk, Sewanee

Farmers National Bank, Winchester, Tennessee

Mr. and Mrs. William Hollis Fitch, Eagle Pass, Texas

In memory of John B. Flynn, Jr., Mobile, Alabama

Mr. and Mrs. Malcolm Fooshee, New York, New York

Frank H. Ford, III, Hattiesburg, Mississippi

Mr. and Mrs. Dudley Clark Fort, Nashville, Tennessee

Mr. and Mrs. Augustus T. Graydon, West Columbia, South Carolina

Mr. James H. Gungoll, Enid, Oklahoma

Mrs. Reginald H. Hargrove, Shreveport, Louisiana

Mrs. Bravid W. Harris, New York, New York

PATRONS

Mr. Howard W. Harrison, Jr., Villanova, Pennsylvania

Mr. and Mrs. R. Morey Hart, Pensacola, Florida

Mr. and Mrs. H. Marsh Henshaw, III, Lake Charles, Louisiana

The Rev. Bertram N. Herlong, New York, New York

Mr. and Mrs. Robert J. Hurst, Port Isabel, Texas

Mr. Charles M. Jackman, Paris, France

Dr. and Mrs. John C. Jowett, Windermere, Florida

The Rt. Rev. and Mrs. Christoph Keller, Jr., Little Rock, Arkansas

Mr. William Ellis Kelley, Fort Lauderdale, Florida

Dr. and Mrs. Charles Briel Keppler, Sewanee

Dr. Edward B. King, Sewanee

Capt. and Mrs. Wendell F. Kline, Sewanee

Don and Em Turner Kuhl, Fort Lauderdale, Florida

Dr. and Mrs. Russell J. Leonard, Sewanee

Anne and Jack Lorenz, Sewanee

Mr. and Mrs. R. Stanley Marks, Montgomery, Alabama

Jim Spearing Mayson, Newport, California

Miss Martha McCrory, Sewanee

Mr. and Mrs. Robertson McDonald, Nashville, Tennessee

Ms. Maury McGee, Sewanee

Mr. and Mrs. Lee McGriff, III, Morgan City, Louisiana

The Rev. W. N. McKeachie, Toronto, Canada

Mr. and Mrs. Arnold L. Mignery, Sewanee

Mr. and Mrs. E. P. Nickinson, Jr., Pensacola, Florida

Mr. and Mrs. Julius F. Pabst, Houston, Texas

Mr. and Mrs. Sam Parr, Jr., Ottawa, Illinois

Maj. Joseph F. Parker, Havelock, North Carolina

The Rev. and Mrs. Henry K. Perrin, Jonesboro, Arkansas

Mr. Eric Lang Peterson, St. Petersburg, Florida

Mr. and Mrs. P. J. Phillips, New York, New York

Mr. and Mrs. Peter R. Phillips, Houston, Texas

Mr. T. T. Phillips, Jr., Jacksonville, Florida

The Very Rev. Joel and the Hon. Mrs. Pugh, Little Rock, Arkansas

PATRONS

Mr. Thurlow Purdy, New York, New York

Mr. and Mrs. Gordon S. Rather, Little Rock, Arkansas

Mrs. Ellen Kirby-Smith Rice, Marietta, Georgia

Mr. Timothy Riordan, New York, New York

St. Michael's Church, New York, New York

Mrs. Eva Gezella Carola Sasdy, New York, New York

Mr. and Mrs. R. P. Shapard, Jr., Griffin, Georgia

Albert P. Spaar, M.D., Charlottesville, Virginia

Mr. and Mrs. Ralph Speer, Jr., Fort Smith, Arkansas

Mr. and Mrs. William M. Spencer, III, Birmingham, Alabama

Dr. and Mrs. John H. Terry, Vero Beach, Florida

Mr. and Mrs. William Dorsett Trahan, Tulsa, Oklahoma

Mr. and Mrs. Henry O. Weaver, Houston, Texas

Mr. and Mrs. R. B. Wilkens, Jr., Houston, Texas

Mr. and Mrs. G. S. Wilkerson, Gainesville, Florida

Mr. and Mrs. James A. T. Wood, Newport, Tennessee